BBQ

The whole hog (all techniques, equipment and recipes)

© Benjamin Bartlett 2012

Published in April 2012

A catalogue record for this book is available
from the British Library

ISBN 978 0 85733 116 8

Haynes Publishing,
Sparkford, Yeovil, Somerset BA22 7JJ, UK
Tel: +44 (0) 1963 442030
Fax: +44 (0) 1963 440001
E-mail: sales@haynes.co.uk
Website: www.haynes.co.uk

Haynes North America, Inc.,
861 Lawrence Drive, Newbury Park,
California 91320, USA

Printed in the USA by Odcombe Press LP,
1299 Bridgestone Parkway, La Vergne, TN 37086

Author	Benjamin Bartlett
Project manager	Louise McIntyre
Designer	Rod Teasdale
Copy editor	Ian Heath
Indexer	Peter Nicholson
Photography	Guy Harrop
	istockphoto.com
	Alamy
	Garden4less
	Macs BBQs
	Dingley Dell Enterprises
	Weber
	Leisuregrow

BBQ

The whole hog (all techniques, equipment and recipes)

Owners' Grilling Manual

A guide to cooking with grills, chimeneas, brick ovens and spits

Benjamin Bartlett

Contents

CHAPTER 1
THE ART OF THE BARBECUE

HOW IT
BEGAN

The barbecue theory of human evolution

Modern barbecuing involves much more than simply applying heat to meat. It's an art form that utilises an open fire to ignite an explosion of tastes offered by meat marinated in spicy sauces, infused with exotic herbs or smoked over aromatic woods. But when and where did it all begin?

In the East African Rift Valley archaeologists have found campfires that are at least 1½ *million* years old. The 'hearth-like depressions' found at Olorgesailie show that our ancestors were enjoying barbecues at the very dawn of time. But that's only part of the significance of these discoveries. In fact without our ability to barbecue we'd probably still be living in trees, eating leaves and picking fleas off each other.

Two million years ago there were two species of ape-like humans living in East Africa. One species, named *Homo erectus* (upright man), discovered fire and used it to cook meat. Meat contains the vital vitamin B12, which doesn't exist in plants, and B12 is essential for building advanced human brain and nerve functions. Thus meat-eating *Homo erectus* developed bigger brains, which helped them survive and eventually evolve into us.

Meanwhile, on the other side of the Rift Valley, a second species of ape-like human, *Australopithecus robustus* (sturdy southern ape), failed to get his fire to light. Australopithecus was consequently reduced to a vegetarian diet of fruit, roots and tubers, failed to develop intelligence and quickly became extinct.

So, the first step along the evolutionary road to modern mankind was the invention of the outdoor grill. But there's another important question to be answered when trying to understand the art of the barbecue: why is it almost always men who do the cooking?

Let's face it, the majority of men in settled relationships wouldn't so much as put a pan on a hob in the kitchen; yet anyone blessed with a Y chromosome is happy to become a god of the gridiron when the cooking equipment is moved outside.

To unravel this particularly knotty mystery we need to look at the primitive religions of the Classical world. Central to many of these (especially in the lands bordering the Mediterranean) was the idea that

For decades and centuries men have been taking over the cooking when it's outside – but why?

the worshippers must share a meal with their gods at least once per lunar month. Of course, the gods couldn't actually turn up at the relevant temple, being too busy chasing nymphs or smiting Midianites, so their share had to be carried up to heaven by smoke. For centuries, therefore, animals were ritually slaughtered and their meat burned on altars to nourish the gods (whence the phrase 'burnt offerings'). More importantly, the priests doing the burning were almost always men.

Anthropologists theorise that such sacrifices evolved from ritualised prehistoric hunts and, for practical reasons, in most human societies hunting is the task of the stronger males. Even today there are hunter-gatherer tribes living in remote corners of Africa and the Amazon jungle where men share the roasted entrails of a kill as part of a male bonding ceremony. Apart from giving the hunters the power of whatever animal they've just killed, this makes the carcass less heavy to carry.

The parallels between these time-honoured rituals and modern barbecues are obvious, so next time your wife complains that you only cook outside remind her that you're simply obeying the laws of human evolution!

There's much debate about the more recent history of this unique method of cooking, with Americans, Australians and South Africans all claiming to have perfected the art of the barbecue. However, most barbecue 'creation myths' begin in the Caribbean. In 1526 a Spanish conquistador wrote that he had witnessed Arawak and Carib islanders drying meat in the sun by hanging it from trees; to keep flies away during the drying process, a smoky fire was lit underneath. The native word for the fire pit used in this method of food preservation was *barbacoa*, hence barbecue.

Another explanation involves the practice of burying a whole pig, goat or other animal in a pit with hot stones or wood embers at the bottom. The heat inside the pit cooks the meat slowly, sealing in juices and tenderising the flesh. These 'earth ovens' were, and still are, used to prepare religious feasts all over the world, and the most famous examples are the Hawaiian *luau* and Maori *hangi*. The indigenous Timucua peoples of South Florida also used sacred cooking pits called *barabicu*.

Still another tale relies on two French words, *barb*, meaning beard, and *queue* meaning a tail (rather than a group of impatient people standing in line). The story goes that when in the 17th century the French conquered the then Spanish Caribbean island of Hispaniola (now divided between Haiti and the Dominican Republic) they discovered the Arawak islanders using a wooden frame placed over an open fire to cook every part of a pig, from 'beard to tail', so nothing was wasted. In French this phrase becomes *barb-à-queue*.

Whilst this story may be a little fanciful, the English word buccaneer, meaning a pirate of the Spanish Main, definitely has its roots in Caribbean cooking. The Arawaks called their wooden cooking frames *buccans* whilst their French conquerors called those who used them *bouccaniers*. English pirate captains, who used *buccans* to feed hungry crewmen burying treasure on deserted islands, became known as buccaneers.

Preparing for a traditional Hawaiian Luau

A more recent explanation of the word barbecue insists that American diners and roadhouses once advertised that they had a pool table with the phrase *Bars*, *Beers and Cues*. As signwriters tend to charge by the letter, this phrase was quickly shortened to BBQ. Unfortunately for fans of this explanation, the *Oxford English Dictionary* credits Somerset-born buccaneer William Dampier with introducing the word barbecue (along with avocado and chopsticks) into the English language in 1697.

Whilst I have no wish to question the scholarship of the *Oxford English Dictionary* there's evidence that people were enjoying barbecues even before Dampier spliced his main brace. A law in the colony of Virginia, dating from 1650, forbids 'the discharge of firearms' at a barbecue.

Americans can take some comfort from first president George Washington, who wrote in his diary for 27 May 1769 that '...I went to Alexandria and enjoyed a barbecue'. Abraham Lincoln also enjoyed outdoor grilling and celebrated his wedding with a barbecue, whilst Thomas Edison designed the first factory to make charcoal briquettes.

Whatever its origins, the art of cooking over hot coals or wood embers has now reached every corner of the world...

A Southern barbecue – back in the good old 1800s

A global gazetteer of barbecue styles

AFRIKANER *BRAAI*

South African barbecuers use a familiar gridiron placed over a metal trough filled with wood embers or charcoal briquettes to cook various types of *vleis* (meat). *Boerewors* (farmer's sausage), *sosaties* (lamb kebabs marinated in fried onions, chillies, garlic, curry and tamarind juice) and *kreef* (crayfish) are particular favourites.

ARGENTINE *ASADO*

At the end of a cattle drive, Argentine gauchos would barbecue huge slabs of beef on an *asado*. Rather than use a rotating spit, which would buckle under the weight of a whole cow, the ranchers of the South American pampas used a large T-shaped metal or wooden frame. The beef is part boned, so it can be splayed, then the front legs of the carcass are fastened to the top crossbar of the T whilst the back legs are secured to a second crossbar at the bottom. The frame is then hammered into the ground at an angle so that the meat is held over the fire to cook. Nowadays smaller *asado* frames are used in back gardens and restaurants to cook poultry, suckling pigs and small joints.

A variation of the above is to cook cuts of beef and other meats on a device called an *asado al disco*, traditionally fashioned from an old plough with four legs welded to the edge. Meat and offal is placed in a spiral around the ploughshare's concave surface so that the dripping fat fries the meat. Peppers and other vegetables are placed at the outer edge so that their juices add further flavour. The *asado al disco* is a griddle rather than a grill and is a popular form of outdoor cooking found all over Argentina, Uruguay, Paraguay and Chile.

AUSTRALIAN BARBIE

A perfect climate, an abundance of fresh ingredients and a love of the outdoors makes Australia the spiritual home of the modern barbecue. Curiously, the cliché of bronzed surfers grilling prawns on Bondi Beach was unknown in Oz until a 1984 advert for the Australian tourist board, in which Paul Hogan encouraged the world to 'slip another shrimp on the barbie'. Urban myths aside, Aussie barbecues range from simple gas grills to glittering stainless steel outdoor kitchens that would make any American barbecuer choke on his Budweiser with jealousy.

CHINESE *CHAR SIU*

To make this classic ingredient for many Chinese dishes, long narrow strips of pork are marinated in a mixture of honey and soy sauce. For a true Chinese-style barbecue the *char siu* is fixed to long skewers and held over glowing coals to cook.

BRAZILIAN *CHURRASCO*

Technically the word *churrasco* refers to grilled beef, but any meat can be part of a *churrasco* barbecue. Brazilian churrascaria restaurants use a theatrical style of serving called *espeto corrido* or *rodízio*, which involves waiters walking around the dining room carrying giant skewers of flaming *churrasco*. The meat is carved at each diner's table and the traditional accompaniment is the *chimichurri* spiced sauce reputedly invented by a British meat importer named Jimmy Curry.

FRENCH/SWISS *RACLETTE*

In days of yore Alpine goatherds tending their flocks would use hot stones from their campfires to melt cheese, which was scraped over bread, potatoes, sausage, ham, gherkins or anything else they had to hand. Nowadays *raclette* dinner parties are popular all over France and you can buy special *raclette* cheese that can be melted in table-top grills with individual *coupelles* (little pans) for each diner.

JAPANESE *TERIYAKI*

The word technically refers to the shine created when meat treated with a *tare* (glaze) is grilled or broiled. The glaze is made by boiling soy sauce and rice wine, either dry sake or sweet mirin according to taste, with sugar or honey. The *tare* is then brushed on to fish or meat before grilling. *Teriyaki* shouldn't be confused with the *teppanyaki* style of cooking, where food is cooked in front of the diners on a large griddle.

GERMAN *SCHWENKER*

This type of barbecue uses a circular gridiron suspended from a tripod over an open fire of beech wood. A *Schwenker* is used to cook the traditional Saarland dish of *Schwenkbraten*, which is pork-neck steaks marinated in paprika and green herbs, eaten with roasted bell peppers and toasted bread rolls.

JAMAICAN JERK

Returning to its Caribbean roots, jerk is a cooking style that uses meat that's been dry-rubbed or marinated with hot 'jerk' spices made from pimento (allspice), Scotch bonnet peppers, cloves, cinnamon, scallions, garlic, nutmeg, thyme and seasoning. Pork and chicken are traditional meats to receive the fiery jerk treatment but fish and shellfish are also popular.

KOREAN *BULGOGI* AND *BULGALBI*

Bulgogi (fire meat) is prepared by marinating beef, pork or chicken in soy sauce, sesame oil, garlic and chilli pepper. The thin slices of meat are cooked on a grill at the diner's table and served with rice and one or more *kimchi* (pickled vegetable) dishes. A variation called *bulgalbi gui*, which means 'ribs grilled over an open fire', is a popular feature of Korean picnics and there are *galbi* restaurants which specialise in this technique in every large town.

MALAYSIAN SATAY

Though commonly associated with Malay cooking, satay is found all over South-East Asia and is an essential item on barbecues from Singapore to the Philippines. In the past any meat was used, including bats, lizards and even elephant, but nowadays only chicken, beef or pork is marinated in the traditional blend of peanuts and curry spices.

MIDDLE EASTERN KEBABS

Found all over the Balkans, the Levant and Iran, the kebab needs no introduction. The poet Homer said Greek heroes besieging Troy ate *obeliskos* (columns) of meat cooked on *krateuta* (skewers), but the word kebab is derived from Persian. The two other words associated with kebab, *shish* and *doner*, are Turkish, but whether you prefer your kebabs skewered or wrapped in pitta bread they're perfect for a BBQ.

MEXICAN CHIMENEAS AND HORNOS

The horno is a beehive-shaped clay oven originating in North Africa and introduced to Mexico by the Spanish. It shouldn't be confused with the free-standing chimenea, which has been used by native Mexicans for heating and cooking since ancient times. That said, both vessels can be used to cook *carne asada* (roast meat) such as the *fajitas* familiar to fans of Tex-Mex cooking, which is the staple food of Mexican picnics called *parrillada*. Another favourite dish is *barbacoa*, which in Mexico should be a whole sheep, slow-cooked over an open fire of mesquite charcoal or in an earth oven. Pork cooked using the *barbacoa* method is called *carnitas*, but in either case the meat is served with soft tortillas, guacamole and salsa.

Left A Mexican horno   **Above A chimenea**

SOUTHERN USA

Barbecuing is practically the national cuisine of America's Deep South. Pork is the meat of choice below the Mason-Dixon Line, except in Maryland, where beef is more popular, and Kentucky, where barbecued lamb is a speciality. The popularity of outdoor grilling in the old Confederacy has produced a bewildering number of local variations but the four main regional styles are:

- **Memphis** – Tennesseans love their pork ribs, which are cooked either wet (brushed with sauce) or dry (rubbed with spices). As an alternative to ribs, pulled pork is served on a bun with coleslaw.

- **Carolina** – the pork can be pulled (shredded) or sliced, but in eastern North Carolina a 'whole hog' must be served with a thin sauce of spices and vinegar, whilst in western North Carolina only the shoulder is used and the sauce is more like ketchup. In South Carolina the signature sauce is either peppery tomato or a mustard-based condiment called 'Carolina Gold'.

- **Kansas City** – confusingly, Kansas City is in the state of Missouri, not Kansas! The city made its fortune shipping meat from ranches in the West to cities in the East so it's hardly surprising that the barbecue is something of an obsession in Kansas City. The unique KC style is based on dry-rubbed meat, smoked over hickory wood and served with a thick, sweet sauce made from molasses.

- **Texas** – the state of Texas is so big it has four sub-styles of barbecue. East Texas style serves chopped (never sliced) beef or pork in a sandwich with a hot tomato sauce; central Texas style originated with German and Czech immigrants and is therefore closer to the European idea of a barbecue buffet; west Texas (cowboy) style uses smoke from mesquite wood to cook goat and mutton as well as beef; and finally south Texas (*barbacoa*) style takes barbecuing back to its roots by cooking a cow's head (*cabeza*) in an earth oven, and serving the shredded meat in a crispy taco shell.

CHAPTER 2
SCIENCE OF THE BARBECUE

A UNIQUE COOKING PROCESS EXPLAINED

Chemistry and physics

If you thought all barbecues were the same, think again. Different types of barbecue actually cook food differently, so before you decide on which type to buy, take a little time to understand what's going on.

www.leisuregrow.com

Besides helping you choose the right style and the right equipment for your needs, being able to explain such things as the Maillard reaction is bound to score a few Brownie points with your fellow barbecue fans. So even if science was your worst subject at school you may be interested in the chemistry, physics and thermodynamics of the barbecue.

THE CHEMISTRY

I doubt if many barbecuers have heard of a 19th-century French food chemist named Louis-Camille Maillard, but whenever people gather to grill they should toast the memory of this great man, because it was Maillard who revealed the scientific secret of the barbecue.

Maillard discovered that certain foods undergo a unique chemical process when cooked. Technically speaking a Maillard reaction is a non-enzymatic oxidisation. Translated for those of us who flunked science, this is what makes food go brown when it's roasted or toasted.

More importantly, different types of food form different flavour compounds during a Maillard reaction. Barbecuing involves a particularly complex Maillard process that bonds protein from meat with sugar from a glaze or marinade. This bonding creates the hundreds of different flavour compounds that are the hallmark of a good barbecue and keep us coming back for more.

THE PHYSICS

For our next lesson we have to move from chemistry to physics, because the critical factor in any Maillard reaction is heat.

In fact the Maillard reaction is extremely sensitive to heat, and different temperatures will produce different flavour compounds in the same food. Therefore because different combustible materials burn at different temperatures, the type of fuel used to barbecue food is very important.

In a barbecue the heat is usually supplied by one of the following:

- **Natural charcoal** – is made from wood heated in low levels of oxygen so that it carbonises but doesn't burn. This process creates a fuel that, if used in a fire with free access to oxygen, burns with a very high temperature. When using charcoal, wait until the flames disappear and each lump is covered with grey ash; this is when the fuel is hot enough to cook the food thoroughly without burning it.
- **Charcoal briquettes** – oddly these rarely contain any natural charcoal! Instead, charcoal briquettes are made by compressing waste material, such as sawdust and coal dust, with a flammable binding agent such as wax. The manufacturing method may be different to natural charcoal but briquettes also produce a powerful heat that's ideal for barbecues. As with natural charcoal, wait until each briquette is coated with ash before beginning to cook.
- **Gas** – the bottled gas used for gas grills is liquefied petroleum gas (LPG). LPG suitable for domestic gas grills is a blend of butane and propane, which are both by-products of the petrol industry. Bottled LPG is readily available from garages, DIY centres and camping stores in a range of cylinder sizes. The main drawback to bottled gas is that the cylinders are heavy and you may be asked to leave a refundable deposit when you buy one.
- **Wood** – burning logs or using a sprinkling of aromatic woodchips can create first-class flavours, but wood on an open fire rarely burns with a flame that's hot enough to cook food quickly and thoroughly. Ovens and smokers cure this problem by concentrating the heat in a cooking chamber and using a chimney to draw more oxygen into the fire.

Besides fuel, the other factor to consider is how to transfer the heat from the fire to the food, and to explain this we have to look at the laws of thermodynamics.

Thermodynamics is the branch of physics that studies how heat is transferred between different objects and materials. For physicists this can be done by radiation, conduction or convection:

- **Radiation** – in this case the term has nothing to do with nuclear power, but describes the waves of electro-magnetic heat energy that 'radiate' from burning fuel. Charcoal grills and open fires cook food by radiation.
- **Conduction** – transfers heat energy from a hot surface to a cold surface by physical contact. The griddle plate on a gas grill or the skillet pan on an open fire cook food by conduction.
- **Convection** – transfers the heat energy from a hot object to a cold object by creating currents in a hot gas or liquid. Casseroles and stews cook food by creating convection currents in the gravy surrounding the food.

As we shall see, brick ovens and smokers are hybrid devices that cook food by a combination of radiation and convection, but let's not run before we can walk. Before we discuss the basic and advanced methods of barbecuing in detail we need to examine the most important debate in modern barbecuing: whether to cook with direct heat or indirect heat.

DIRECT HEAT VERSUS INDIRECT HEAT
In brief, the difference between direct and indirect heat is:

- **Direct heat** – a charcoal grill or open fire cooks by direct heat, by constantly exposing the food to heat radiating from burning fuel.
- **Indirect heat** – flat griddle plates, skillet pans and other such cooking vessels cook food by indirect heat, because there's a metal plate or other surface between the fuel and the food.

So which is better? In practical terms the advantage of using indirect heat is that the hot metal plate conducts heat evenly over the entire cooking area, so that wherever the food is placed the inside starts to cook before the outside burns.

On the other hand the advantage of using direct heat is that it maximises the effects of the Maillard reaction. The direct heat of a charcoal grill or open fire creates 'flare-ups', which are caused by melted fat dripping on to the hot charcoal and bursting into flame. These flare-ups lightly char the edges of the food, and it's this 'char-grilling' that enhances all the flavours produced by Monsieur Maillard's reaction. Indirect heat doesn't produce this effect.

The great debate
A brief guide to the different types of barbecue

Nothing splits the normally amiable and friendly brotherhood of the BBQ like the argument between direct and indirect heat. Charcoal grillers insist that direct heat is the original, and therefore the only authentic, way to barbecue. On the other side of the divide gas grillers think devotees of charcoal are stuck in the Dark Ages, eating blackened burgers and raw sausages in some outdated ritual related to ancient fire worship.

A classic gas barbecue from Leisuregrow

Of course, these opinions are extreme, and there are plenty of compromises that let gas grillers recreate that heavenly char-grill taste and allow charcoal grillers to eat something that hasn't been turned to pure carbon in the flames. Nevertheless, the debate over direct and indirect heat goes on and before a beginner can begin to barbecue they have to pick a side, since choosing a side will affect what type of barbecue you'll enjoy using. If you're a traditionalist who likes to get their hands dirty then direct heat from a charcoal grill is definitely for you. Alternatively if you like quick, clean and convenient cooking then a gas grill's indirect heat may suit you better.

To further complicate the basic choice, we also have to consider the various outdoor ovens and back garden smokers that are now available for domestic use. Admittedly smokers and ovens are advanced forms of barbecue that use a mix of both direct and indirect heat to cook food, but before you make your final choice take a look at this brief guide to grills, ovens and smokers.

CHARCOAL GRILLS

Someone recently asked me why bother to go to all the trouble of cooking outside when most modern houses are equipped with a perfectly good kitchen cooker that almost always has a gas or electric grill attachment?

The answer is that there's a crucial difference between an indoor kitchen cooker and an outdoor charcoal grill, and that's the position of the heat source. With an indoor kitchen cooker, the grill attachment cooks food from above (called broiling in the US) at very high temperatures, but an outdoor charcoal barbecue cooks food low and slow from beneath. Applying direct heat from above also means there are no flare-ups, so much of the flavour from the meat juices is lost, but cooking from underneath allows the juices to fall on to the hot charcoal or briquettes and ignite. The smoke from these flare-ups infuses food with all those fabulous flavours.

Similarly you can't burn aromatic wood on a gas or electric indoor grill. Sprinkling chips of hickory, pecan, mesquite, maple, oak or apple wood on to the glowing embers of charcoal gives food that wonderful wood smoke flavour, and using different proportions of these woodchips lets you create your own unique BBQ style.

If you decide the charcoal option is right for you, there are plenty of different designs from which to choose. There are permanent brick barbecues (built from scratch or bought in DIY kit form), long metal troughs designed for larger parties and German-style hanging baskets. But for simple family barbecues in the back garden you can't do better than a classic 'kettle' style.

The kettle grill was designed to be cheap to buy and easy to use and was invented in 1952 by an American sheet-metal worker named George Stephen Sr. Stephen worked for a Chicago company called Weber Brothers Metal Works which, among other things, made metal buoys for the harbours of Lake Michigan. At this time all domestic barbecues were either permanent brick structures or temporary lash-ups cobbled together from steel oil drums cut in half.

One blustery weekend in the Windy City's suburbs, Stephen became fed up with gusts blowing ash from his brick barbecue on to his hot dogs and decided to do something about it. Next day at work he cut an old harbour buoy in two, welded three legs to the lower half, turned the upper part into a lid and separated the two hemispheres with a grating.

Stephen's neighbours mockingly christened his invention the 'Sputnik' (because of its remarkable resemblance to the USSR's spherical satellite) but he had the last laugh. His grill was so successful that Weber Brothers Metal Works soon became the Weber-Stephen Barbecue Products Co. Weber-Stephen still make a superb range of kettle grills, widely available from good garden centres and DIY stores. Inevitably there are cheaper kettle grills

An original Weber kettle barbecue from the 1950s

than an original Weber, but with barbecues, like everything else, you get what you pay for.

Once upon a time all you could do with a charcoal barbecue was grill, but now there's a huge range of accessories that let you roast, bake and braise. There are even motorised spit rotisseries and automatic kebab turners!

Recently invented Grillstream Technology Barbecues help prevent flare-ups and stream the fat away, and are available in 360° charcoal grills or ready-fitted to Leisuregrow gas barbecues.

Design options

A modern Weber kettle barbecue

Remember, your grill will be subjected to fierce heat when in use and bitter cold when in storage, so any model you choose needs to be robust and sturdy. Also, to get the most from the opportunities offered by kettle and other designs of charcoal grill you need to choose a design with:

- **A lid** – essential for a number of advanced barbecue techniques, acts as a windshield on blustery days and keeps the elements out when not in use.
- **Adjustable vents in the lid** – these will help you regulate the amount of smoke and heat coming into contact with the food, creating a range of flavours to suit different tastes.
- **Wheels and handles** – when you need to store the grill in the shed or move it to a more sheltered spot, wheels and handles will help you manoeuvre the grill around easily.
- **Wooden side shelves** – to hold food, tools, pans and other paraphernalia.
- **Easily removable racks and accessories** – the easier such items are to remove, the easier they are to clean.

Everything but
the kitchen sink

GAS GRILLS

The Weber-Stephen charcoal grill didn't have a monopoly on back garden cooking for long. In the early 1960s a new kid on the barbecue block appeared: the propane-powered gas grill.

The domestic outdoor gas grill was invented by William G. Wepfer and Melton Lancaster, who worked for the Arkansas & Louisiana Gas Company. Wepfer's job was to find new ways to sell LPG to the public and he thought bottled propane would be an excellent barbecue fuel. He and Lancaster consequently began tinkering with an old charcoal grill, and after a few false starts the back garden gas grill was born.

Apart from the fuel used, the principal difference between gas and charcoal grills is how they apply heat to the food. As we've seen, charcoal grills use direct heat from the glowing embers of solid fuel, but most modern gas grills use indirect heat to cook the food.

The food is placed on a metal plate heated from below by propane-powered burners. The heated cooking surface can be smooth or ridged, the former being called a griddle and the latter a grill pan. The ridges of a grill pan are supposed to lift the food away from the melted fat so that it 'grills' rather than 'fries'. Most modern gas grills offer a combination of griddle and grill pan to create a more versatile cooking area.

The principal advantages of using gas griddles or grill pans is that food placed at the edge of a hot plate should cook at the same rate as food placed in the middle, and there are no holes to let smaller items fall through into the flames. Another advantage is that they offer an easily lit, easily controlled heat source that cooks food quickly and safely, so no messing about with dirty coals or dangerous lighter fluids!

As I've already mentioned, diehard guardians of the charcoal flame can be a little snooty about gas grills. These direct-heat purists claim that because the griddle's indirect heat eliminates the flare-ups that are the key feature of charcoal grilling, gas-grilled food lacks an authentic 'flame-grilled' taste.

As a response to this criticism some models of gas grill now offer vaporiser bars as a standard feature or optional accessory. Vaporiser bars fit over one or more burners of the gas grill and are used with an open grate. The burners heat the bars, and the fat from the cooking food drips on to them to vaporise and flare just like a classic charcoal barbecue.

With or without vaporiser bars, gas grillers can recreate the wonderfully complex flavours found in campfire cooking by using herb brushes, spice rubs and marinades (see Chapter 5).

If you decide that the gas option is right for you, you should choose a device that's the right size for your needs. In general you need more burners for more people, and the usual rule is to double-up on your average-sized party, for example, two burners will cook for at least four people, three burners will cook for at least six people and four burners will cook for at least eight people. For larger event catering Crown Verity barbecues, available from R.H. Hall, are made from commercial grade stainless steel and fire up quickly, reaching high temperatures in just a few minutes.

Besides a choice of burners, even inexpensive gas grills now offer an impressive array of gadgets. These include electric rotating racks for kebabs, side burners to heat sauces and side dishes, and warming plates to keep food hot. Top of the range gas grills now feature ceramic or infrared spit rotisseries, just like the ones in a kebab shop, but as with charcoal grills you should look for a few key features when buying your first basic model (see the panel on page 27).

DISPOSABLE GRILLS

Incredibly the disposable barbecue actually pre-dates the modern gas grill and kettle charcoal grill. Today's throwaway cookers have evolved from the military hexamine cookers invented in Germany in 1936.

A modern hexi-cooker uses hexamine (a solid fuel similar to paraffin wax) to cook the food. Hexamine tablets are easy to carry, ignite and store, but the food cooked on such devices tends to have a distinct chemical taste.

The lack of a flame or glowing coals makes these disposable grills ideal for battlefield use, but civilian versions of the hexi-cooker are available from specialist camping shops. Wherever lighting a normal barbecue is impractical a hexi-cooker may be the answer, but in most ordinary picnic situations a simple disposable charcoal barbecue is a better option.

The throwaway charcoal barbecue consists of a foil tray containing charcoal briquettes impregnated with a lighting agent, and a wire mesh on which to place the food. Easy to use, highly portable and relatively cheap, these are an ideal way to barbecue on the beach or any place where you can't take your trusty back garden grill.

The principal drawbacks of throwaways are a lack of versatility and their small cooking area. Don't expect to do anything other than grill with direct heat, and you may need three or four disposables to feed a hungry family.

SMOKERS

The very first barbecues were simple log fires, and any food cooked over burning wood will automatically absorb some of the smoke to create a natural smoky flavour. Unfortunately heat from campfires is very difficult to control and this means the outside of food can be burned black whilst the inside is left raw and full of harmful bacteria.

The ideal way to create an authentic campfire flavour, whilst cooking food all the way through, is to use a device with a more controllable source of heat and smoke – namely a smoker.

A smoker uses a wood fire or propane gas to heat a pan containing damp woodchips. The heat and smoke produced by the smouldering chips of hickory or other aromatic woods cooks the food, kills nasty bugs and adds flavour. The heat inside the smoker has to be kept low to stop the woodchips from bursting into flame, and this is done by excluding oxygen and/or placing a pan of water between the food and the woodchips. Because the water and woodchip pans separate the food from the heat source the smoking method is sometimes called 'indirect grilling'.

There are a number of different designs of smoker, which I'll discuss in more detail in Chapter 5. Here it suffices to say that barbecuing with smoke can impart wonderful flavours and tenderness to food, but because of the low temperatures involved you do need several hours to cook food properly.

Furthermore, a bit of practice and preparation is required to get the best results from smokers. Some food needs to be pre-soaked in brine (brining), and you need to ensure that the smoke can move around inside the smoker when the door's closed. Stale, stagnant smoke deposits tar and other unwanted chemicals on to the food, creating a taste of industrial creosote rather than rural campfires.

Impatient barbecuers wanting smoky flavours without the wait could pre-cook food on the kitchen hob and finish it off outside in the smoker, but this is cheating and the results are rarely satisfactory. If you need quick, low-maintenance barbecue food a back garden smoker is probably not for you, but if you have the time to experiment and practice a smoker will provide many hours of culinary fun.

The good news is that if this form of barbecuing is for you, most good garden centres now sell all the equipment you need, including a range of bagged woodchips that make taking up smoking a lot easier!

A Kamado ceramic coated sxmoker

Back garden ovens

Besides charcoal grilling and wood smoking, other forms of early barbecue used earth ovens to bake food. These simple holes in the ground, filled with hot embers and food wrapped in green leaves, slowly evolved into the brick ovens and chimeneas used since ancient times and now seen in back gardens all over Europe and the Americas.

The difference between a brick oven and smokers is that with an oven the burning wood is placed inside the cooking chamber then removed once the required temperature has been reached. The walls of the oven are designed to retain the heat from the 'firing' and release it slowly to cook the food. This retained heat method is perfect for roasting meat and cooking casseroles, as well as baking breads, pizzas, and cakes.

The principal disadvantage of brick ovens compared to gas or charcoal grills is that they're more costly to construct and require a lot more time and effort to use. Free-standing Mexican chimeneas are much cheaper to install than a permanent brick oven but even these require some skill to keep the cooking area at a constant heat. In other words, practice for a bit before inviting the whole neighbourhood round for a chimenea pizza party!

Grilling whatever the weather
Alternatives to outdoor grilling

In inclement summer weather, or once winter holds our nation in its icy grip, I've seen desperate barbecuers move the grill into their garage. However, it should be obvious to anyone that using a building designed to store cars and lawnmowers as an emergency barbecue pit is downright dangerous. Besides the serious threat of carbon monoxide poisoning, most garages (mine included) are crammed with old tins of paint, cans of petrol and other containers half-full of highly flammable material. I'd therefore strongly urge every barbecuer to resist any temptation to grill in the garage during wet weekends.

Equally I'd never grill underneath one of those foldaway gazebos or garden awnings, because these canopies are usually made from highly flammable synthetic materials. If rain clouds appear halfway through cooking I encourage my guests to congregate under the gazebo whilst I carry on grilling in the rain ('bracing', as my old Dad liked to describe it).

So if we can't grill in the garage or under a gazebo, and the rain threatens to move beyond 'bracing' to extinguishing mode, what are we to do when the storm clouds gather?

You can try and avoid the problem arising by keeping an eye on the weather forecast, but weather forecasting isn't noted for its accuracy here or anywhere else in the world. In fairness to the meteorologists, of course, no long-term forecast can predict the weather with absolute precision, but short-term forecasts for the following two or three days can actually be quite accurate. But no matter where you live, no weather prediction can ever be 100% correct, so if – despite checking the forecast every five minutes – your chosen barbecue day is still too wet to cook outside you can always try a grill designed for use indoors. A skillet is ideal (see below) or you could opt for an indoor or 'hot rock' grill (see opposite).

Use a skillet to grill it

The alternative to an indoor or hot rock grill is to use your kitchen hob and a cast iron skillet pan to recreate the tastes of genuine campfire cooking. The trick is to not merely fry the food in the skillet – you also need to use herb brushes, spice rubs and marinades to give your food that true BBQ flavour.

Flat-bottom skillet pans have a younger sister in the form of the ridged grill pans that have become increasingly popular for 'healthy' frying. Both these pans are excellent substitutes for the outdoor grill, but, as we saw earlier, there's a scientific reason why they can't match the taste of food cooked on a proper outdoor charcoal barbecue: they use a different physical process to cook the food, and it's understanding this difference that will help you make the right choice when it comes to buying a barbecue.

INDOOR GRILLS

There are a growing number of devices being marketed as indoor barbecues, most of which fall into one of the following two categories:

- **Contact grills** – like sandwich toasters, contact grills have electric heating elements in both the base and the lid to cook food from above and below. When the lid is closed, both sides of the food are brought into contact with the hot cooking surfaces, hence the name.
- **Open grills** – these have an electric element in the base only, and an open grate for the cooking area. Food is placed on the grate to be cooked from below by the hot element.

These devices cook food very well, but the sad truth is that they don't do much more than your existing kitchen stove. Nor can such indoor barbecues reproduce the char-grilled taste of cooking over an open flame, because they don't have an open flame.

You can get closer to an authentic barbecue taste by using a skillet pan (see below), but if you want to provide indoor food with the same spontaneity and party spirit as an outdoor barbecue I'd suggest investing in a hot rock grill.

GET YOUR ROCKS HOT

The hot rock grill is similar to the Alpine raclette, which uses a table-top electric element to melt cheese placed in little pans. With a hot rock grill the grooved metal cooking surface of the raclette is replaced by a slab of granite that's heated to the required cooking temperature by the electric element. The hot rock will then cook food placed directly on it or below it in little pans.

You can still prepare the food to be cooked using the rubs and marinades that are such an important part of outdoor dining. When everyone is seated, each guest can sear their own beef, tuna or salmon steak, cook a kebab or roast sliced vegetables according to their taste. The indoor hot rock grill thus recreates the communal atmosphere of the back garden barbecue without endangering life and limb.

The best hot rock grills come complete with little grill pans that can be placed underneath the stone, and a 'gravy groove' around the edge of the granite to stop dripping juices ruining your best Irish linen tablecloth.

HOW TO CHOOSE A BARBECUE GRILL THAT'S RIGHT FOR YOU

Which grill to go for

Hopefully you're now an expert on barbecue fuels, styles and equipment! However, there are a couple more factors you need to consider before buying a barbecue:

- **Skill** – it makes sense for beginners to start with a simple gas or charcoal grill barbecue to refine their skills before tackling more advanced equipment such as smokers and wood ovens.
- **Commitment** – if you don't want to spend all afternoon bent over the barbecue, choose the simplest gas grill you can find.
- **Practicality** – There's no point in having a wood-fired oven if you live in a smoke-free zone. Equally, there's no point in buying a massive eight-burner grill if you only ever cook for two or three people.
- **Storage** – don't forget to consider where you're going to store everything. Unless you have plenty of willing sons and daughters who are happy to help you lift heavy equipment, choose a cart-style gas or charcoal grill. Cart or trolley barbecues are fitted with wheels and usually have a storage area underneath for gas cylinders and other accessories. This means they can be moved in and out of your garage or garden shed with ease.
- **Budget** – you can spend anything from £20 to £10,000 on barbecue equipment. I'm not kidding. Beefeater, an Australian BBQ company, offers its top of the range 'Signature Outdoor Kitchen Centre', made of weatherproof stainless steel, for a cool AUS$50,000; that's about £20,000.

With these factors in mind, take a look at the following chart, which summarises the pros and cons of each barbecue style and device:

This gas barbecue is ideal for up to 12 people

www.leisuregrow.com

A classic charcoal barbecue is fine for 4–5 people

Device	Advantages	Disadvantages	Ideal for
Charcoal grill	■ Authentic BBQ tastes. ■ Real 'Theatre of Barbecue'. ■ Cheap to buy. ■ Fuel is cheap and readily available.	■ Takes time to light and for the fuel to reach the right temperature. ■ Difficult to control heat levels. ■ Very variable temperatures across the cooking area. ■ Difficult to clean. ■ Bags of fuel are heavy, messy and dirty.	■ Beginners and serious barbecuers wanting to give family, friends and small parties a traditional barbecue experience for very little cost.
Gas grill	■ Easy to use – just switch on and light up. ■ No mess, no fuss. ■ Highly controllable heat levels. ■ Temperature distributed evenly over entire cooking surface. ■ Very versatile – lots of gadgets offer a wide variety of cooking options.	■ Food lacks authentic flame-grilled flavour. ■ More expensive to buy and run than a charcoal grill. ■ Gas cylinders heavy and difficult to store.	■ Beginners and casual barbecuers who want to entertain family, friends and larger parties.
Disposable barbecue	■ Easier to light and less messy than conventional charcoal grills. ■ Highly portable. ■ Cheap to buy.	■ Heat levels difficult to control. ■ Small cooking area – you may need several to cook for a family. ■ Food can have a slight kerosene taste. ■ Not very versatile – can grill effectively but no more. ■ Environmentally unfriendly.	■ Camping, fishing, picnics and other trips where you can't take a proper charcoal grill.
Wood fire smoker	■ Fabulous range of traditional flavours.	■ Takes time to prepare and for fuel to reach the right heat levels. ■ Takes several hours for food to cook. ■ Difficult to control heat levels. ■ Can be messy and dirty.	■ Skilled barbecuers or beginners prepared to practise.
Propane gas smoker	■ Fabulous traditional flavours. ■ Easier to use than a solid fuel smoker. ■ Faster cooking times.	■ More expensive to buy and run.	■ Any barbecuer wanting to explore new techniques, but best avoided by complete beginners.
Permanent brick oven	■ Fabulous flavours. ■ Very versatile – can be used to prepare a wide variety of foods. ■ Real 'Theatre of Barbecue' effect.	■ Takes time to prepare. ■ More expensive to buy/build. ■ Some skill and practice required to use properly.	■ Larger gardens or patios, and serious barbecuers.
Free-standing chimenea	■ Cheap to buy. ■ Easier to use than a brick oven. ■ Very versatile – can cook breads and pizzas as well as grill meat. ■ Can provide a source of heat if the night turns chilly.	■ Some practice required to use properly. ■ Requires regular sealing to prevent cracks. ■ Can be messy, especially to light and clean out ashes.	■ Smaller gardens, and barbecuers prepared to practise to get the best results.

Do-it-yourself barbecues
How to build permanent back garden grills and temporary campfires

An alternative to buying a free-standing metal barbecue is to build your own bespoke grill from bricks or other masonry.

There's a growing number of companies offering DIY kits. All the preformed component parts, including masonry and ironwork, are delivered on a pallet, so all you have to do is choose an appropriate site (see 'Playing with fire' at the end of this chapter), mix the cement and put it together.

Because the non-metallic parts are usually made from reconstituted stone (a mix of crushed stone and cement that can be easily moulded into different shapes) the end product is called a masonry barbecue. They can look good, but even basic models can cost several hundred pounds. If budgets are limited a cheaper option is to build your permanent grill from good old-fashioned house bricks.

Unless you're a qualified gas fitter you should restrict yourself to building a brick grill for natural charcoal and briquettes. That's the bad news. The good news is that even if you've never laid a brick in your life, you should be able to build this simple permanent grill in less than a day.

YOU'LL NEED THE FOLLOWING:

- **Materials** – approximately 200 clean house bricks, mortar (water, sand and cement). Plus chippings and plaster sizer for concrete base if required. Metal strips (for trays and racks to sit on).
- **Tools** – a spade, shovel, bricklayers' trowel, bricklayers' spirit level, wheelbarrow (or large board) to mix cement, a piece of 2x1 for a gauge rod, a tool (or short length of hose) to neaten mortar joints.
- **Accessories** – a barbecue grill set containing a steel grill for cooking and a pan for charcoal (available from most garden centres and DIY stores). We got ours from Black Knight (www.blackknightdirect.co.uk)

Plan your barbecue position (ideally a sheltered spot away from the house, garage, shed and overhanging trees but close enough to the kitchen). Build it at a comfortable working height; ask your local builders' merchant to help you work out the exact number of bricks you'll need. Make a note of which layer of bricks you need to add in the metal strips or bricks for the trays.

Step 1 If you are not building onto an existing concrete or stone surface, mark out an area slightly larger than the finished BBQ.

Step 2 Use a sharp spade to remove the turf.

Step 3 Dig out to approx 10cm and flatten out the soil.

Step 4 Mix up enough concrete to fill the trench, level off and leave to set for at least 48 hours.

Step 5 Using the cooking tray as a template, lay out the first course of bricks.

Step 6 Put a spirit level up against the bricks and then remove the line of bricks and mark the position on the base. Repeat this for the other two lengths.

Step 7 Mix some mortar (five parts sand to one part cement and add water until the mix becomes stiff but workable). Spread the first layer of mortar directly on to the base where the first course of bricks is to be laid.

Step 8 Put the first brick in position.

Step 9 Then add a small amount of mortar to the end of each brick and work along the line.

Step 10 Use your trowel to tap the brick into position.

Step 11 Lay further courses of bricks, making sure alternate vertical joints overlap by half a brick. Check the vertical and horizontal levels regularly.

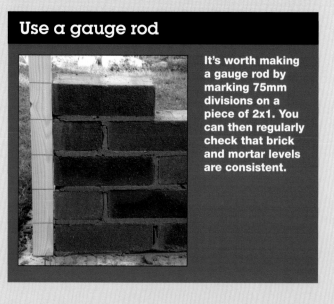

Use a gauge rod

It's worth making a gauge rod by marking 75mm divisions on a piece of 2x1. You can then regularly check that brick and mortar levels are consistent.

Step 12 Cut bricks in half to finish off the end of a course.

Step 13 When you reach the level for the first tray, position the metal strips and check there's enough overhang for the tray to rest on. Instead of using metal strips, you can lay bricks at 90° to create a ledge for the trays.

Step 14 Add mortar on top of the metal and continue with the next course.

Step 15 Check all your levels one last time, tapping down where necessary.

Step 16 Finish by running along the mortar joints with a suitable tool to neaten them off.

Step 17 But make sure you leave it until it's nearly dry before you brush off any loose mortar (otherwise you'll mark the bricks).

Picnic barbecues and lash-ups

If you need something temporary and portable for a picnic barbecue you can always improvise. Remember Mr Stephens and his navigation buoy? His invention of the kettle grill proves that any fireproof container can be turned into a solid fuel grill.

A makeshift grill is called a 'lash-up' by the serious barbecue fraternity, and the only rule is to make sure that whatever you use as a fire pan can be operated safely. Other recommendations include:

- If you've cut an old oil drum in half, file down any sharp edges.
- If you fit legs make sure they're strong enough and stable enough to carry the fire pan when fully loaded with fuel and food.
- The container must be thick enough to withstand high temperatures without buckling or melting.
- The interior of the container must be clean.

Using a gridiron saves your food from dropping into the fire

Whatever you use for a fire pan, it's worthwhile investing in a couple of gridirons to hold the food clear of the fuel.

A true gridiron has only horizontal parallel bars whereas a true grill has horizontal and vertical bars, but let's not split hairs. What you need is something with two metal grates joined by a hinge at one end and fitted with insulated handles at the other.

Gridirons are designed to keep food from falling into the fire and will help you turn everything easily; they can be used with any type of barbecue but are particularly useful for lash-ups and campfires. Simply place your chicken wings, steaks, sausages and burgers between the two frames and when one side is done turn it all over using the handle.

Campfire barbecues

A campfire under the stars is really getting back to your barbecuing roots, but if you're planning a barbecue picnic in the countryside, or on the beach, make sure campfires are allowed before striking your first match. In dry weather temporary bans on campfires may be in force, especially on highly flammable heathland and moorland areas, so please check.

Besides giving your guests a truly memorable barbecue experience your goal should be to leave no visible trace of a fire after you've gone home. Wherever you're planning to cook, dig a shallow hole for the fire and keep the earth or sand handy to put back later and to use as a fire extinguisher in case of an emergency. If cooking on grass, cut away a suitable area of turf and keep it on one side to put back later.

Now ring the edge of your impromptu fire pit with good-sized stones to stop rogue sparks spreading the fire; but never take stones from a wall, even if you intend to put them back.

Whilst you do all this, send the kids off to gather firewood. Naturally you'll need a range of stick sizes from twigs to start the fire to thick logs for the cooking, but instruct your eager beavers to bring back only dry deadwood, and tell them that the largest log should be no thicker than your arm. Build the core of the fire with dry leaves and add a pyramid of sticks around it. Start with thin twigs and build up to the thicker logs. You should then be able to start your fire with one match applied to the dry leaves.

Now comes the cooking. You could use the old woodsman's method and fashion a spit from two forked tree branches, pushed into the ground on either side of the fire; but a much better way is to use the gridiron you bought for your last lash-up.

As with charcoal barbecues you should never use the flame for cooking, as this will simply burn the outside of the food whilst leaving the inside raw. Instead, wait until the flames die down and you have a good pile of red-hot embers.

Rake the ash into an even bed, place the food in the gridiron and support it on the stones around the edge. You can also wrap potatoes, sausages and corn on the cob in foil to bake in the embers, but remember to retrieve these items with tongs to avoid burnt fingers!

When you've finished cooking douse the fire with water, and when the embers are cold replace the sand, earth or turf you removed earlier. Take all your litter home and never leave the site until you're absolutely certain the fire is 100% out.

Use stones to contain a campfire

Playing with fire
How to ensure you have a safe barbecue

Nothing demonstrates a man's democratic right to do what he likes with his property more than lighting a fire in his back garden, but sadly barbecues aren't popular with local fire brigades or hospitals. I'm sure freedom-loving firefighters and medical staff enjoy a flame-grilled burger as much as anyone, but every summer increasingly scarce public resources are diverted to dowsing garden sheds and garages set on fire by badly-sited barbecues! Similarly, A&E departments across the country spend many hours treating barbecue burns that are usually entirely preventable. So before we go any further in this book, let's look at some simple steps you can take to prepare yourself, your family and your garden for a safe barbecue.

www.leisuregrow.com

STAND FIRM
If you haven't built a permanent barbecue pit make sure whatever grill you're using is placed on a firm, level surface that's sheltered from strong draughts. You can create a suitable stand for your barbecue very cheaply with a couple of flagstones bought from your local DIY store or garden centre.

BRIGHT SPARKS
Even if you're using a gas grill, there's a danger of rogue sparks being blown under eaves or into other dangerous places. To avoid turning your potting shed into a bonfire of your barbecuing vanities, make sure your grilling area is at least 7.5m (25ft) from your house, shed, greenhouse, garage, fences, overhanging trees, hedges, piles of dry leaves and anything else that may be a fire hazard. Similarly, ensure your grill is sited well away from any parking area, as hot ashes falling on the bonnet rarely improves the appearance of a car.

FIRE STARTER
Of course, we want to start a fire, but only one that we can keep under control, so never use petrol, paraffin or any other flammable spirit, as these ignite with a highly dangerous flare. If you want to keep your eyebrows, and the respect of your guests, always use proper BBQ lighter fluid and follow the manufacturer's instructions carefully.

When preparing the grill, use gloves to handle coals, briquettes, firelighters and fluid, otherwise all your food will taste of barbecue fuel rather than your secret sauce recipe! Once you start cooking, use oven gloves and long-handled tongs to avoid nasty burns, and remember to use separate tongs for raw and cooked meats.

KIDS' STUFF

Children are fascinated by fire, so kids need to be kept well away from a hot grill. If you have toddlers and young children coming to your barbecue why not make a simple fireguard from chicken wire (plastic coated to avoid scratches) and garden canes? Simply thread the canes through each end of the chicken wire and at regular intervals, then push the canes into the lawn around the barbecue to create a fenced-off area. This exclusion zone should have at least 1m (3ft) of space around all sides of the grill so that you can move around your barbecue freely.

Tie flags or bunting securely to the tops of the canes both for decoration and so that people can see the barrier. When you're finished, simply roll everything up and store it in the shed for next time. If you don't have a lawn, push the canes into large plant pots filled with sand or soil. These pots can also be used as fire extinguishers in an emergency.

Whilst we're on the subject of fire extinguishers, you must have some method of putting out the flames quickly. Besides buckets of sand, soil and water for wood and charcoal grills you can buy suitable fire extinguishers for gas barbecues from good garden centres, DIY stores and specialist BBQ suppliers. It may seem

www.leisuregrow.com

obvious, but remember that no form of fire extinguisher is any good if it's left in the kitchen, so keep it close by.

Finally, no grill should be left unattended, not even for a moment. If you have to nip inside to get more chicken wings from the fridge make sure someone sober is on hand to keep an eye on things in your absence.

Further important safety advice can be found in the next chapter.

Crazy but true!

The following moment of BBQ madness was related to me by a friend whose parents were very keen on caravanning.

At the end of one especially enjoyable family holiday, the grill-master in question decided to have one last barbecue before heading for home. The evening went well, the burgers never tasted better, the sausages were especially succulent and the party lasted long into the night.

The following morning the family were awake bright and early to pack up and leave the campsite. The previous night's barbecue had been so perfect it seemed a shame to waste the half-burned briquettes lying in the fire pan so our hero carefully wrapped these leftover coals in newspaper and put the parcel inside his caravan.

Halfway up the motorway the caravan burst into flames. Though the coals had felt cold the newspaper had insulated the charcoal so effectively that there was enough heat to reignite them! Happily the family escaped without serious injury, but their caravan was completely destroyed.

The moral of this cautionary tale is to make sure your barbecue has been properly extinguished when grilling has finished for the day – and never put hot coals in your shed, house or caravan!

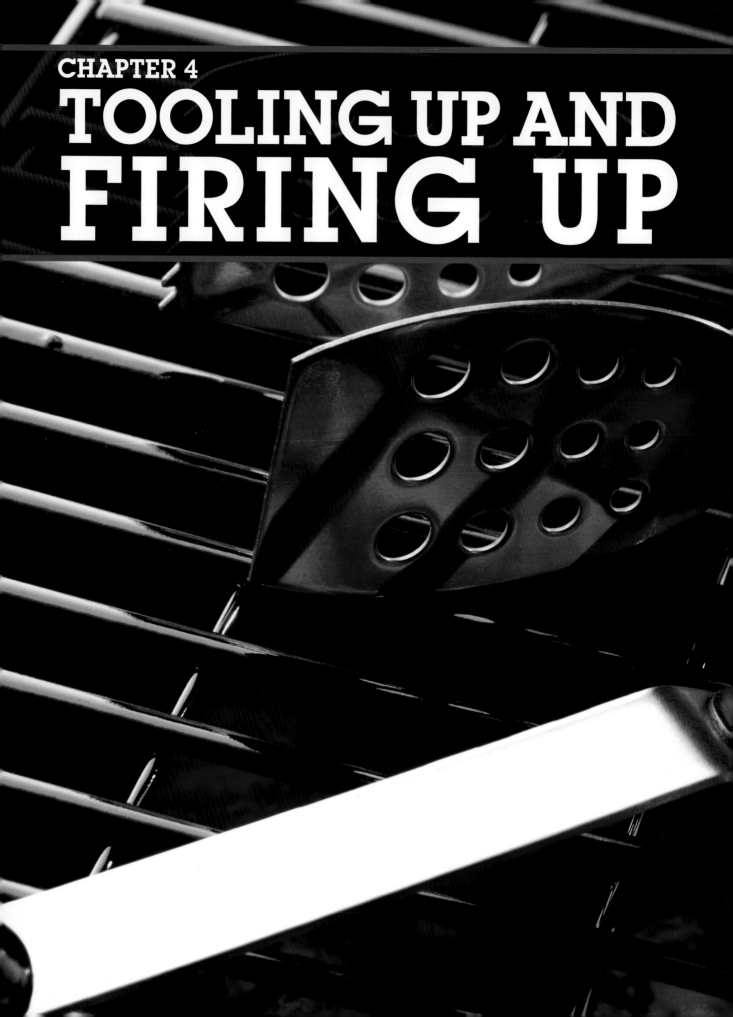

CHAPTER 4

TOOLING UP AND FIRING UP

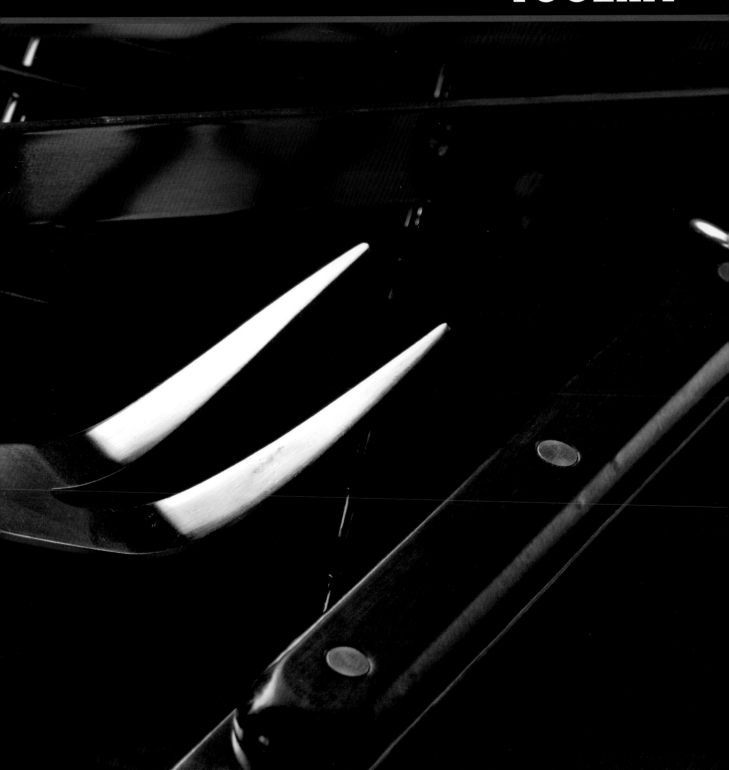

A GOOD BARBECUE CHEF NEEDS A GOOD BARBECUE TOOLKIT

Tools of the trade

The ability to use rocks and sticks as tools helped our ape-like ancestors evolve into modern man. Primitive stone tools were so important to early humans that they acquired a religious significance and were often buried with their deceased owners.

Fast forward several millennia and the implements may have changed but man's ancient rapport with his tools has not. Just as our prehistoric campfires have evolved into the barbecues of today, so the flint axes used by our Stone Age forefathers have become the skewers and spatulas used by modern grillmasters. So a man's tongs and carving fork aren't just functional instruments to flip burgers and turn sausages, they're a spiritual link to his hunter-warrior past.

A quick scan of barbecue blogs on the internet or the grill aisle at your local garden centre will illustrate exactly what I mean, because both the names and the design of barbecue tools are always unashamedly masculine.

Take the 'Gangster BBQ Set'. This fine 12-piece example of the tong-maker's art comes in a polished rosewood carry-case that resembles the 18th-century boxes containing a gentleman's duelling pistols. Similarly, the 'Gadget Man BBQ Set' comes complete with its own foam-lined, brushed aluminium case similar to the ones used by TV camera crews in war zones. My favourite name, however, is the 'Grillslinger Barbecue Belt', which has Wild West-style holsters to hold the tools. Such names neatly encapsulate a man's special relationship with his barbecue tools.

But as Shakespeare might have put it, what's in a carry case? The best case in the world is nothing more than an empty box if the tools inside aren't up to the job.

Any quality tool perfectly combines innovative design and precision engineering to help its owner perform a practical function, and a good barbecue tool is no exception. Of course, you could spend any amount of money on grill accessories, but the bottom line is that all your barbecue tools should do one or more of the following:

- Help you cook better.
- Protect you while you cook.
- Protect the food while you cook.

So in the light of these requirements, let's take a look at the essential items you'll need in your barbecue toolkit.

A professional barbecue toolkit

The tools you need

First of all, don't raid the kitchen drawer for tongs, spatulas and other equipment, as indoor versions of these tools will rarely be suitable for outdoor use. What you need are extra-long utensils with insulated handles and heatproof blades, as these will help to keep frail human flesh from being scorched by the flames. So if you don't want your food to taste of singed body hair, choose proper barbecue versions of the following:

SPATULA

The 10cm (4in) blade of a standard spatula is ideal for flipping burgers, steaks and chops, but I'd also invest in an extra-wide spatula with a 45cm (17in) blade, such as the GrillPro Professional, for turning fish and other large items easily and efficiently.

Besides regular spatulas, there are a number of combi-spatulas available that incorporate several different tools in one utensil. Like Swiss Army knives, these hybrid-spatulas feature such built-in implements as serrated edges for cutting and slicing and even a bottle opener for the busy barbecuer to open his beer. Personally I like to keep one tool for one job, since this not only prevents cross-contamination but also allows me to buy more tools!

FORK

A two-pronged fork is a highly useful tool, and not just for retrieving sausages that have fallen into the fire. A fork can test chicken joints to ensure juices run clear, prick sausages, and hold food for slicing. The two-pronged fork is preferable to three-pronged varieties because two tines can be more easily extracted from the item being held.

As with tongs, it's vital to have at least two colour-coded forks and use one for raw food and the other for cooked food.

TONGS

These are vital for turning sausages, chicken drumsticks and other cylindrical items that have a nasty habit of rolling off a spatula or getting stuck to a fork. Choose a design with handles at least 40cm (16in) long and with a locking mechanism that'll grip food without you having to exert constant pressure. Besides allowing you to place items precisely on the cooking area, locking tongs avoid the problem of accidental early release whereby sausages and burgers end up in the fire rather than on the grill.

You should always have at least two sets of tongs with colour-coded (or easily distinguished) handles. Use one set for handling cooked food and the other set for raw food. This will prevent food-poisoning bacteria that live in uncooked food from contaminating cooked items.

KNIFE

Like a soldier and his rifle, the true chef has a special relationship with his knife. It should be sharp enough to slice and dice finely as well as robust enough to chop and cleave through bone and gristle. During an afternoon of heavy grilling your knife will have to work as hard as you do, so it's worthwhile investing in the best blade you can afford.

One of the chief mistakes made with knives is to over-sharpen the cutting edge. Swishing the blade rapidly up and down your sharpening steel, like Blackbeard honing his cutlass, may look impressive but this sort of display actually achieves very little. In fact so-called sharpening steels don't sharpen a knife blade at all. To sharpen a dull edge properly you need a good whetstone that will gently grind away a few microns of metal to produce a keen edge. After this process, you use a steel to straighten the edge created by the whetstone.

The secret to using steels or whetstones is to treat each side of the blade evenly and to hold the blade at the correct angle while doing so:

How to use a steel

- **Hold the steel downwards with the point resting on a suitable firm surface, like a chopping board.**
- **Place the knife across the steel at an angle of approx 20° from the vertical, with the butt of the blade (the part closest to the handle) touching the steel.**
- **Draw the blade gently back towards you, from handle to tip, whilst gliding the whole blade down the whole length of the steel.**
- **Repeat ten times, then do the same on the other side of the knife and steel.**
- **Wash and wipe the blade clean of any tiny pieces of metal that may contaminate food.**

Once again, it makes sense to have at least two knives, colour-coded for raw and cooked food.

15-20°

1 2 3 4

BASTING BRUSH

The secret of successful barbecuing is the application of spices, sauces, rubs and marinades, so having spent all Saturday morning preparing your special sauce it makes sense to apply it with a proper heat-resistant basting brush designed for the job.

A traditional basting brush has a wooden handle and pig-hair bristles, but these natural materials can trap bacteria and aren't dishwasher-proof. Most modern indoor and outdoor chefs therefore prefer a basting brush with a dishwasher-safe synthetic handle and silicone hairs.

At the beginning of the barbecue season give basting brushes an anti-bacterial soak in sterilising fluid suitable for babies' bottles or home-brewing equipment. Wash the brush thoroughly after each session and repeat the sterilising process every few weeks during the season.

GRILL-CLEANING BRUSH

Stale grease and burnt fat clinging to your grill or griddle will taint the taste of food during cooking, so you need a proper cleaning brush to remove these contaminants. Choose a design with heatproof wire bristles, a long handle made of wipe-clean plastic and a scraper to shift stubborn baked-on food.

This tool should also be used during cooking, to clean food scraps from the cooking area so that your chicken doesn't taste of steak or your sausages of grilled peppers and so on. It shouldn't be confused with the short-handled cleaning brushes used for intense cleaning when the grill is cold (see also 'Cleaning afterwards' later in this chapter).

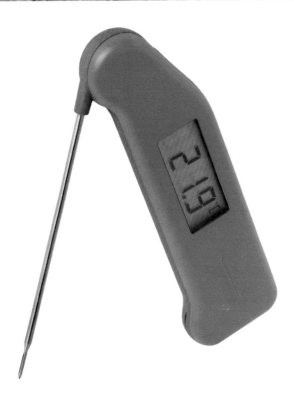

My favourite is the SuperFast Thermapen thermometer, which gives you an accurate reading in less than four seconds. Coming with its own water-resistant case, the probe folds away for safe storage and is available in a range of colours.

For grillers who love gadgets there are barbecue forks with built-in food thermometers. However, the latest device to take the barbecue tool market by storm is the digital infrared thermometer gun. These high-tech temperature gauges, originally designed to help firefighters find hotspots in the wall cavities and roof voids of smouldering buildings, detect the infrared light radiating from cooked food and display the result on an LCD screen. The advantages of these contact-free guns are that they're easy to use – just 'point and shoot' – and there's no probe to push into semi-cooked food. The disadvantage is that they're quite expensive.

DIGITAL THERMOMETER

I can't say often enough that the biggest threat to a perfect barbecue isn't the weather, or the neighbours complaining about the smoke – it's trying to cook food at the wrong temperature. (For correct cooking temperatures see Chapter 4.)

As we all know by now, unpleasant food-poisoning bugs live in all uncooked food, including vegetables, and partial cooking can make matters worse. This is because partial cooking can raise the temperature to a point where these bugs will happily multiply to dangerous levels. Only complete and thorough cooking will kill E. coli and salmonella, so to be absolutely sure your food is 100% safe you need not one, but two good thermometers: an equipment thermometer and a food thermometer.

An equipment thermometer will accurately measure the temperature inside your smoker, oven or grill. Some grills and smokers have built-in thermometers, which are fine for checking the heat has reached the required level to start cooking, but frequent opening of the hood can seriously affect their readings. A safer alternative is the dedicated equipment thermometer with a probe designed to sit inside the grill, oven or smoker. The best designs also have a multi-function timer and can withstand temperatures up to 370°C (700°F).

Equipment thermometers can help you cook better because they give accurate cooking temperatures for your grill, griddle, oven or smoker, but for food hygiene purposes you also need a food thermometer to measure the temperature of the item being cooked. Food thermometers use a temperature probe that's pushed into the food at periodic intervals, so to prevent cross-contamination be sure to wipe the probe clean, preferably with an anti-bacterial wipe, after each use.

OVEN MITT

Unless you have asbestos fingers an insulated oven glove is essential to avoiding a Sunday afternoon in A&E. Indoor oven gloves are often too thin to be much good outdoors, so I'd choose a gauntlet design specifically made for barbecues. These should have extra insulation to protect your hands and lower arms when handling hot grills and pans. My personal favourites are Gloven heat-resistant oven gloves that can withstand high temperatures.

The tools you don't need – but are fun to have

Barbecuing isn't just a method of transferring food from the fridge to the human stomach; it's also a fascinating hobby that can get you and your family out into the fresh air (weather permitting), reduce your stress levels (children permitting), and provide hours of innocent pleasure (neighbours permitting).

Like golf, fishing and any other hobby, half the fun is choosing the right accessories to make the whole process run more smoothly and successfully. There's an ever-expanding range of non-essential barbecue extras which can help you get more from your grill, and if your other half objects to you spending money on any of the following, just point out that your hobby is a lot cheaper than building a model railway, taking up sailing or buying a share in a racehorse (etc etc etc).

APRONS

Besides offering an opportunity to display a gallimaufry of bad barbecue puns ('Hail to the Chef', 'Licensed to Grill', 'King of the Grill', 'Commander in Chef', 'Grill Sergeant', 'Do Your Wurst', 'Ladies Love Big Meat', and so on), today's specially-designed BBQ aprons do much more than protect your clothes whilst cooking. Nowadays the best grilling aprons come with tools fitted into tailored pockets so that everything wraps into a neat roll for easy transport and storage.

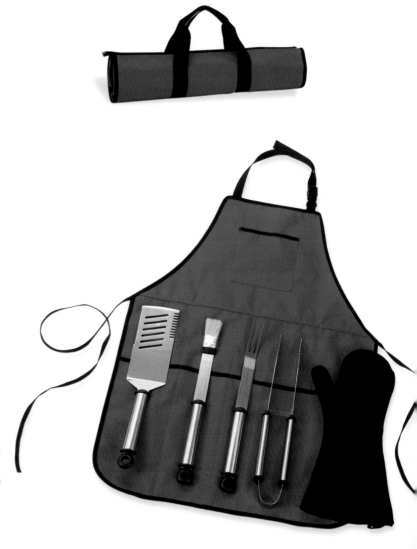

BARBECUE COVERS

If your grill is destined to live outside, a hardwearing cover will reduce the damage caused by rain/sun/snow and add years of life to your beloved barbecue equipment. Don't try and make do with a bin bag or plastic builders' sheet, because proper tailored covers to fit kettle grills, trolley grills, brick grills, chimeneas, wood ovens and even spare gas bottles cost just a few pounds and are readily available from good barbecue equipment suppliers or on the Internet.

CAST IRON SMOKER POTS AND STAINLESS STEEL SMOKER BOXES

These simple metal containers allow aromatic pellets and woodchips to smoulder without the need for pre-soaking. Because they release more smoke for longer, these devices give food a fuller flavour. However, whilst most models can be used with both charcoal/gas grills and smokers you should always check before you buy.

COMBINATION AND MULTI-TOOLS

I've already mentioned that these days you can buy combination tools that incorporate just about every possible barbecue gadget in one device. To take just one example, the Flameboy BBQ Multi-Tool is a single-handled implement that contains a spatula, fork, tongs, bottle-opener, corkscrew, serrated cutting edge and even a little pocket for a disposable lighter.

I've also already mentioned that I like to have a separate tool for each different job, but I do keep a multi-tool in the glove compartment of my car so that I always have what I need to cook on a campfire!

CORN COB HOLDERS

Short skewers for holding corn on the cob will stop butter dribbling over your fingers. However, they can be a real pain to clean, so choose a set that's dishwasher safe.

CLIP-ON LAMPS

An adjustable, battery-operated, clip-on lamp is a real help when grilling after sunset and will help preserve that romantic after-dark atmosphere.

FISH HOOKS

Essential for smoking fish as well as catching them! Fish hooks fix in the top of your smoker so that fish, chops and other food can hang in the smoke. This allows the smoke to penetrate deeper into the meat over a wider surface area, so creating a fuller flavour.

MARINADE INJECTOR

Like many 'short cuts', a marinade injector can't compete with a proper marinade of 24 hours in your special sauce. However, if you have to barbecue quickly, or if you forgot to marinade your meat the night before, a marinade injector is an excellent emergency substitute.

SAUSAGE HOLDERS AND GRILL BASKETS

There's nothing more annoying than seeing a lovely Lincolnshire sausage roll slowly off the grill into the charcoal below. Even prompt rescue by tongs, forks or spatulas can't revive the unfortunate banger's delicate flavour; but burnt sausage misery can be a thing of the past if you use a sausage holder. This clever little gadget is a simple gridiron with four or more semicircular slots to hold and turn sausages easily.

The same principle applies to grill baskets, which are designed to let you cook chicken wings, chillies, onion rings and other small items without them slipping through the bars of the grill. Available in square or circular shapes, and in a range of sizes to fit most barbecues, grill baskets can be a real boon if you're cooking for a large number of people, because they also make handy trays for carrying food from the grill to the table.

Oil sprayers and misters

For applying apple juice, olive oil, glazes and thin bastes evenly you can't beat a proper aerosol-free mist sprayer, and do I need to say never use a sprayer that's previously held a household cleaner? Good.

PIZZA PANS AND PIE IRONS

Special BBQ pizza pans let you cook fresh or frozen pizzas on a standard charcoal or gas grill without the need to build a wood oven. Charcoal grillers can also cook your favourite pies to perfection with a set of pie irons. Just pop your pie into the moulded iron pan, close the lid and place in the embers of a hot barbecue – but make sure you grease the pie pans first to avoid the pastry sticking to the metal. You can also use pie irons to bake campfire bread and other small items.

ROTISSERIES

If your charcoal or gas grill doesn't have an integral rotisserie you can always buy a spit-roast attachment. Choose a model with four-prong spit-forks (the prongs ideally spaced about 3in apart) to hold food securely, a battery-operated motor with a counterbalance to reduce motor wear, and an automatic reverse feature that will rotate food anticlockwise as well as clockwise.

ROAST AND RIB RACKS

A close relation of the toast rack, the rib rack is designed to hold ribs, chops and chicken portions vertically in the flames. Their advantage is that they create more room on the cooking area, but you do need to turn the items more often to ensure even cooking.

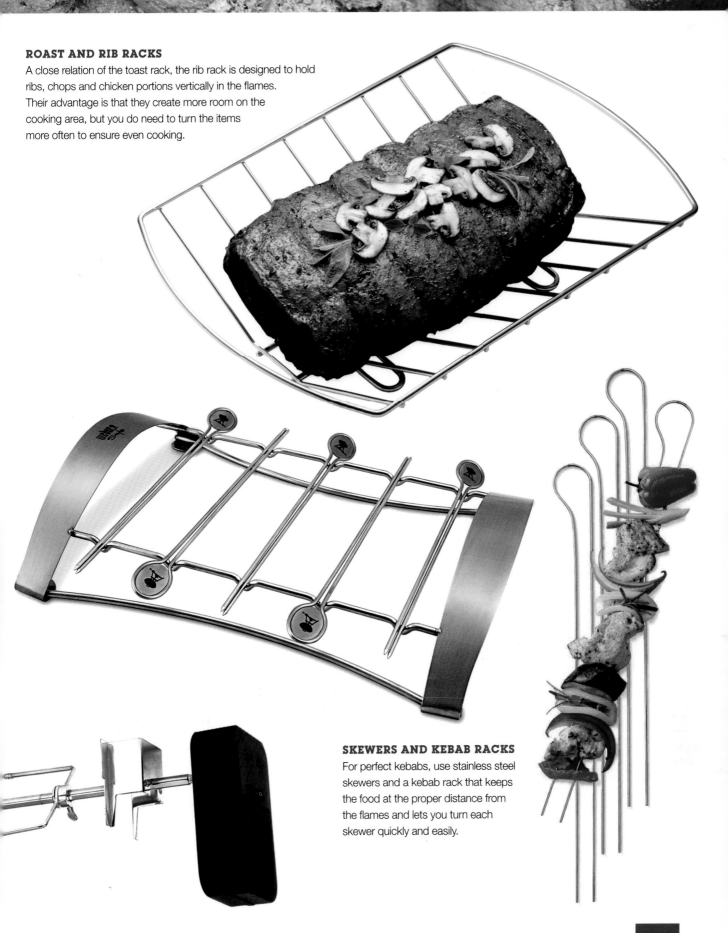

SKEWERS AND KEBAB RACKS

For perfect kebabs, use stainless steel skewers and a kebab rack that keeps the food at the proper distance from the flames and lets you turn each skewer quickly and easily.

Light my fire

Simple steps to getting your barbecue started

Gas grillers can comfortably skip this section, because all they have to do is turn on the gas and light the burners with a long-handled match, safety splint or electronic spark gun. Users of brick ovens, smokers and charcoal grills, on the other hand, have to make more of an effort to get their barbecues going. But more effort produces more reward. So if you've ever used an entire box of matches to light your barbecue, this next section is for you.

MATCHES AND CIGARETTE LIGHTERS

If you use matches or a cigarette lighter don't try to light the charcoal, wood or briquettes directly. Remember, matches burn too quickly to light a briquette properly and the metal parts of a disposable lighter can get incredibly hot if the flame is lit for more than a few seconds. I've seen more than few burned fingers and thighs caused by returning a disposable lighter to a pocket before it's cooled down!

Rather than risk permanent scarring, twist a page of newspaper lengthways, hold it downwards in a gloved hand, light the far end with your match or lighter and then hold it against the barbecue fuel. If it burns too short, extinguish it by putting it in the bucket of water you previously placed nearby (see page 50).

LIGHTER FUEL

Briquettes should light easily without the need for lighter fuel because they already contain an accelerant. However, if they've been exposed to the open air for any period longer than a few days all the accelerant will have been neutralised by the oxygen in the air, so you'll have to add more in the form of a suitable lighter fluid.

Be sure to choose a fluid specifically designed for barbecues, always follow the manufacturer's instructions, and always ignite fluid-soaked fuel at arm's length (preferably whilst wearing safety gloves and goggles). Also, never use domestic firelighter tablets, as these can give your food an unpleasant chemical taste.

GAS LIGHTERS

A proper gas lighter is by far the best way to light barbecue fuel. Most models are powered by a disposable butane container designed for refilling cigarette lighters, and the best designs have a childproof safety lock, extra-long 11in reach and a controllable flame.

BBQ BLOWER FAN

To speed up bringing charcoal to the required cooking temperature a number of wind-up and battery blower fans are available. The best one is the Jundor BBQ Bellows that runs on a 3V motor and a couple of batteries and can prime a barbecue in less than five minutes. It acts like a bellows, supplying air and oxygen into the coals with a long metal tube, and the eco-friendly side of it means you don't need firelighters, lighter fluid or impregnated charcoal.

CHARCOAL CHIMNEY STARTER

One of the drawbacks of charcoal grills is estimating the initial amount of fuel needed and the time it will take for the coals to become hot enough to cook, but both these problems can be solved with a charcoal starter.

A charcoal chimney starter is a simple metal cylinder, closed at one end, with holes at the bottom and a handle on the side. These handy gadgets are designed to help you light and heat charcoal and briquettes to the right temperature quickly and without the need to pile them in a neat pyramid.

They're cleaner and easier to use than fistfuls of grubby charcoal. Just roll a page of newspaper into a doughnut, place this paper ring in the bottom of the metal cylinder, fill with the coals and light the paper. In 20 minutes you should have perfect glowing coals with no mess and no fuss.

Five easy steps to lighting a fire

Of course no man needs to be taught how to light a fire. Thousands of years of evolution have hardwired fire-lighting into male brains, and we all have our own favoured methods. But that said, sometimes we all need a little refresher course:

1 Make sure your wood, charcoal or briquettes are bone dry. If you're opening a fresh bag of fuel there should be no problem, but if you're using last season's coals that have been over-wintering in a damp garage or shed, or logs from a wood pile exposed to the elements, the chances are that the fires of hell won't get your grill to light. If you do keep charcoal or briquettes for long periods between barbecues store them in an airtight plastic container.

2 If you can, choose a sheltered spot to set up your grill. Avoid places such as the gap between two houses, which can funnel and magnify the tiniest of drafts into a howling, match-snuffing gale.

3 Remove all ash, and for a standard-size charcoal barbecue build a pyramid of approximately 30 briquettes in the centre of the fire pan. For larger grills build several pyramids along the length of the trough. This simple step is often ignored because of the mess involved, but a pyramid shape is absolutely crucial to getting your grill going. If you don't like dirty fingers, keep a gardening glove handy and/or invest in a charcoal starter (see below).

4 For natural charcoal grills and wood ovens you should build your pyramid around a core of several pages of newspaper scrunched into a ball, and layer the structure with smaller sticks/charcoal pieces closest to the paper and larger logs/charcoal pieces on the outside.

5 Once you have your fuel properly arranged you can apply the necessary naked flame. Apply it at different points around the pyramid to ensure an even flame; and to avoid burning yourself, start at the point furthest away from you and work backwards.

Finally, it has to be said that however difficult the fuel is to light never douse it in petrol, paraffin, kerosene or any other high octane accelerant. The flash fire from even a small cupful of petrol can reach 50ft into the air and travel much faster than you can duck.

Cleaning up afterwards

There's no way round it, sooner or later you'll have to roll up your sleeves, fill a bucket with water and break out the brushes. This is thanks to Isaac Newton's Third Law, which states that every action must have an equal and opposite reaction, which proved that our universe is a duality of conflicting opposites. In barbecuing terms this fundamental law of physics means that all the fun of the fire has to have a downside, and that downside is cleaning.

I'm afraid there's no substitute for hot soapy water and elbow grease when it comes to cleaning any barbecue, but the following may be of some help:

TOP TOOLS FOR CLEANING GRILLS

- **A soft bristle brush and olive oil** – coating grills and griddle plates in olive oil helps prevent food from burning and sticking to the metal so that cleaning afterwards should be easier.

Use an old basting brush to apply the oil liberally to all parts of your cooking area before you begin to barbecue, and use a mist sprayer to reapply oil during cooking.

- **A hard wire brush** – a stiff wire brush specially designed for grill cleaning is invaluable for cleaning cold grills. The best cleaning brushes are the triangular three-in-one designs that feature a wire bristle brush, a wire wool scourer and a metal scraper for really tough areas.

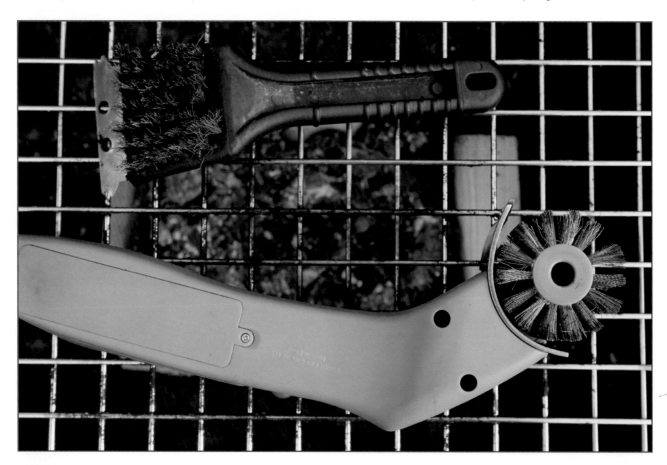

■ **Grill stones** – grill stones are specially designed to get grease and baked-on grime off your grill. They look like bathroom pumice stones but have a long handle to make scrubbing a little easier.

TOP METHODS FOR CLEANING GRILLS

■ **Soaking** – place the removable parts of your grill's cooking area in warm (not hot) water with a little vinegar or dishwasher detergent (choose one or the other, don't use both). Such a soaking should loosen stubborn dirt and food, especially from hard-to-reach areas such as the edges of racks and grills.

■ **Baking** – for really gunky charcoal and gas grills, light up, close the lid and let the baked-on food scraps burn away. Once the grease and grime has been transformed into ash it should be easier to remove with your wire brush or grill stone.

■ **Chemical** – various chemical cleaners specifically designed for barbecues are available. Most brands use caustic soda (sodium hydroxide) to remove grease and dirt. This is highly toxic and irritating to human skin, so wearing gloves is a must. There are non-caustic brands available but gloves should be worn even with these. After using any chemical cleaner rinse all parts of the grill thoroughly in clean water to avoid contaminating the food.

Top tips for cleaning grills

■ **Never mix cleaning products, as the combination of chemicals can produce a cloud of chlorine gas. If you have any doubts about the dangers of chlorine remember that this highly toxic chemical was used as a lethal weapon during World War One!**

■ **Before using any cleaning product or method check both the product and the grill manufacturer's instructions to make sure you won't damage the equipment or void the warranty.**

■ **Clean the cooking areas as soon as possible after use. If the metal is still warm it will be easier to clean, as the carbonised food won't have had time to harden; but check that parts are cool enough to handle safely before touching them.**

■ **Always clean your grill before use as well as after. Dust, spiders and insects can all find their way through the tightest-fitting cover, but a quick wipe down will keep unwanted bugs out of your burgers.**

■ **If your barbecue still smells of stale grease after a good clean, mix two teaspoons of bicarbonate of soda (baking powder) in a large cup of water and use a cloth to wipe the mixture over the whole grill. Finally rinse away the mixture with clean water.**

When barbecues go bad
Fire and first aid emergencies

Even the best-run barbecues and most experienced barbecuers will occasionally have to face an emergency. If a rogue spark sets light to the lawn or someone cuts themselves on a broken glass, as host and head of the family you should be prepared.

Of course, in really serious emergencies you must call the appropriate emergency services, but you can prevent a minor problem becoming a major crisis by taking a few simple safety precautions.

 Fire safety dos and don'ts for barbecues

Some of these safety tips are mentioned elsewhere in this book, but it does no harm to repeat them:

Dos
- **ALWAYS place the grill on a flat stable surface at least 7.5m (25ft), or as far away as you can, from the house, garage, shed, fence, decking or any other flammable structure, and well away from overhanging trees and piles of leaves.**
- **ALWAYS use just newspaper or a charcoal starter to light a fire.**
- **If you do use a starter liquid, ONLY use fluids recommended for barbecues and ONLY apply it to cold coals.**
- **ALWAYS keep children and pets away from the grill area at all times.**
- **ALWAYS keep your grill clean by removing grease and fat, as this will help prevent flare-ups and flash fires.**
- **ALWAYS keep charcoal, spare gas cylinders, starter fluid, matches and any other flammable material out of the reach of children and well away from any naked flame or source of heat.**
- **ALWAYS let the coals cool completely when you've finished cooking and dispose of any ash or unburned fuel in a metal container.**

Don'ts
- **NEVER leave your grill unattended.**
- **NEVER use a gas or charcoal grill indoors.**
- **NEVER grill under the influence of alcohol.**
- **NEVER use a gas grill with a leak.**

CHECKING FOR GAS LEAKS

At the start of each season check everything for leaks. Brush soapy water on to the gas hose and the connections then turn on the gas – a leak will cause bubbles. If you detect a gas leak, by smell or the soapy water test, turn everything off and have the appliance serviced by a professional before using it again.

If you smell gas while cooking, get everyone as far from the grill as possible and call the fire brigade; do not move the grill.

FIRE EXTINGUISHERS

My old scoutmaster used to say you should never start a fire unless you know how to put it out, and I've known older barbecuers keep a large box of baking powder by their grill to use as an emergency fire extinguisher.

Whilst bicarbonate of soda may have been the only solution in the early days of back garden grills, nowadays there are plenty of fire extinguishers specifically designed for outdoor use.

The important thing to remember is never to chuck a bucket of water over a barbecue that's burning out of control, because the resulting cloud of scalding steam can be just as dangerous as the flames. Instead, keep the following items handy:

- A metal bucket full of sand.
- A powder or foam fire extinguisher suitable for both charcoal and gas grills.
- A large kitchen fire blanket.
- A metal bucket full of cold water.

The bucket of cold water can be used to extinguish matches, tapers and splints safely at the start of the cooking session and cool down hot grills, griddle plates and other tools at the end.

The best way to extinguish a charcoal or wood barbecue fire after cooking has finished is simply to close the lid and let the fuel burn itself out. However, if you have to extinguish the embers quickly use a pair of old tongs to place each hot coal in the sand bucket and cover them with more sand. You can retrieve the coals later by using a garden sieve.

Coals can still be very hot even when they look cold, so leave any used fuel to cool properly overnight – or for as long as possible – before handling.

FIRST AID FOR CUTS, BURNS AND SCALDS

Barbecues get hot. *Very hot.* This may seem obvious but many people can forget this basic fact once they get caught up in the fun and frolics of a good barbecue. It's so easy to grasp a hot metal grill with an ungloved hand or skewer ourselves with a kebab whilst cooking outside that it makes sense to keep a good first aid kit handy and learn some basic guidelines for treating burns and cuts:

FIRST AID KIT

Naturally, prevention is better than cure, so always wear gloves and use long-handled tools when lighting, tending and cooking on a barbecue. However, in order that you can treat a minor injury if one should occur you need to have a good first aid kit to hand, which should contain the following:

- Sterile burn dressings.
- Sterile burn gel.
- Surgical tape.
- Latex gloves.
- Bandages.
- Low-adherence dressing.
- Sticking plasters.
- Antiseptic ointment.

MINOR BURNS AND SCALDS

- Cool the burn as quickly as possible with clean, cool water, but do not use ice or iced water, as it's too cold.
- Burns should be cooled for at least 10 to 30 minutes.
- Forget what granny told you – NEVER apply butter or cream to a burn, as this will actually fry the skin and spread the wound.
- You can apply a cooling gel specifically designed for burns and scalds.
- Apply a sterile dressing.

MAJOR BURNS AND SCALDS

- If clothing has caught fire, extinguish the flames with water or by smothering with a blanket, but do not put yourself at risk.
- Call an ambulance immediately.
- While you're waiting for help to arrive, and if you can do so safely, remove any clothing or jewellery around the burnt area.
- Do NOT attempt to remove anything stuck to the burn, as this could make matters worse.
- Cool the burn with cool or lukewarm water for 10–30 minutes. As with minor burns, never use ice, iced water, creams or greasy substances such as butter.
- Keep the patient warm. Cover him or her with a blanket or layers of clothing but avoid the injured area. Rapid cooling can send a person into shock, especially if you're cooling a large burn and/ or the patient is very young or elderly.

- Cover the burn with a layer of cling film, but don't wrap it around a limb. A clean, clear plastic bag can be used to protect burns to a hand or foot until specialist help can be found.
- The pain of minor and major burns can be treated with paracetamol or ibuprofen. Always read the label when using any medicine and remember that children under 16 should not be given aspirin.

MINOR CUTS

- Wash the wound to remove any dirt or debris, but do not use soap.
- If bleeding is heavy apply gentle pressure to each side of the cut.
- Bleeding should stop after about ten minutes. If it doesn't, seek medical advice.
- Apply an antiseptic ointment.
- Apply a sterile dressing.

MAJOR CUTS

If the cut is very deep and/or the bleeding is very heavy the wound may require stitches and a tetanus injection, in which case you must call an ambulance or take the patient to hospital. You can try to staunch the flow of blood by applying gentle pressure to each side of the wound and/or covering with a clean absorbent material but...

- Do not try to clean a major wound.
- Do not remove impaled objects (such as skewers and forks).
- Do not try and remove deeply lodged debris.
- Do not breathe on an open wound.
- Do not push back exposed body parts.

If you're in any doubt about the correct treatment of any wound or injury you must seek proper medical advice as soon as possible.

⚠ Other emergency equipment

Besides something to extinguish fires and a first aid kit you should also keep the following handy:

- **Safety goggles – to use when lighting the barbecue.**
- **Safety gloves – even after the fire is out the metal parts of a barbecue can remain surprisingly hot for a surprisingly long time. If you have to handle metal parts after cooking has finished always use safety gloves.**
- **A metal container with a tight-fitting lid – for storing lighters and matches.**
- **A torch – a good barbecue will always go on long after night has fallen!**

CHAPTER 5
BASIC BARBECUE TECHNIQUES

THE SIMPLE SKILLS YOU NEED TO COOK BRILLIANT BARBECUES

Food safety and hygiene

Everyone enjoys a good barbecue, and by everyone I don't just mean people. Salmonella, E. coli, campylobacter and a whole army of other nasty microbes love to feast on grilled food, and these are the bugs that can cause food poisoning.

Chronic diarrhoea and vomiting would ruin anybody's weekend, but the risk of food poisoning can be reduced dramatically by proper storage, careful preparation and thorough cooking. So before exploring the different techniques of barbecuing with charcoal, gas and smoke, let's remind ourselves of the basics of food hygiene.

KEEP IT CLEAN

You should also follow these simple food hygiene rules before, during and after using your grill:

- Never grill on a dirty grill. Whether you use charcoal/briquettes or gas, give all your fire pans, burners and cooking surfaces a thorough scrub at the start of the season and a good wipe down before each use.
- Always wash your hands thoroughly after touching raw or uncooked food.
- Never put cooked food on a plate or other surface that's been used for raw food.
- Keep raw meat in a sealed container away from cooked meat and other items that are ready to eat, such as salads and bread buns.
- Don't put raw meat next to cooked or partly cooked meat on the grill.
- Don't use sauces or marinades on cooked food that have been previously used with raw meat.

KEEP IT COOL

Food must be stored at the proper temperature before it's cooked. This is especially important during the summer because bacteria like to breed in the warm sun.

Bacteria will grow rapidly between 4°C (40°F) and 60°C (140°F), so you need to avoid this dangerous 'Goldilocks Zone' where the temperature is just right for multiplying microbes.

You should keep the food you're going to cook on the barbecue below 4°C. So if you don't want to be running back to the fridge every five minutes, keep your meat in sealable, airtight containers inside an insulated cool box. Besides keeping everything fresh a cool box will keep insects, pets and other unwanted diners away from your steaks, sausages and burgers until you're ready to cook.

Colour-code cooking utensils

This recipe contains raw eggs. Of course, you're using decent quality free-range eggs, aren't you? Good. Also bear in mind that pregnant people should keep well clear of all raw eggs, due to the potential salmonella risk. Best keep Junior safe.

The biggest threat to our digestive systems comes from the bacteria that live in raw meat and uncooked food. Proper cooking will kill these bugs, but you must also prevent cooked food from being recontaminated by coming into contact with raw food.

To avoid the dangers of cross-contamination, all raw and uncooked food – not just meat – must be kept separate from cooked food by storing it in different containers and handling it with different utensils.

In the heat of a good barbecue it can be difficult to remember which tongs, knife, basting brush or chopping board has been used for which food, but this problem can be cured by using colour codes. Commercial kitchens now use a standard colour coding system of:

White – bakery and dairy.
Green – salad and fruit.
Red – raw meat.
Yellow – cooked meat.
Brown – vegetables.
Blue – raw fish.

Few of us can afford to own six different sets of equipment but you must have at least two sets of utensils, containers and chopping boards, one colour-coded red for raw food, the other yellow for cooked.

If you're going to cook any frozen items you must also make sure that all frozen food is properly thawed before cooking. The best way to thaw frozen food is to place it in your fridge for at least 24 hours, or until all the ice crystals have melted, but make sure that melted ice can't drip on to other items in the fridge. Never thaw food outdoors or in hot water, and if you use a microwave for defrosting you must cook the item immediately.

Don't forget that extras such as green salads, rice salads, dips, dairy products, mayonnaise, cold meats and desserts must also be kept cool until you're ready to eat. Providing your buffet table is kept out of direct sunlight, perishable food can be left for up to two hours, but only one hour if the day is very hot and the temperature rises above 30°C (86°F).

You may be surprised to see rice and other non-meat items listed in the previous paragraph, but a remarkable number of food poisoning cases are caused by eating reheated rice and/or unwashed vegetables. The plain fact is that any food can harbour harmful bacteria, so all food should be kept cool and washed thoroughly before cooking and serving.

KEEP IT HOT

At the other end of the thermal scale is the need to keep cooked food warm. If you're cooking for large parties and you need to keep a lot of food warm, you must ensure that its temperature doesn't fall below 60°C (140°F). Some barbecue designs, especially the more expensive gas grills, feature built-in warming racks. Alternatively, for a modest sum you can buy a proper stainless steel food warmer called a chafing dish (from the French word chauffer, meaning to warm), which is a hot water bath consisting of a frame, with or without a lid, holding a large pan for the water and a second smaller pan, or pans, to hold the food. A spirit burner under the large pan

keeps the water hot and the hot water keeps the food in the small pans warm without burning or drying out.

Hotels and restaurants use chafing dishes for breakfast and other buffets but they're also readily available from good cook shops and websites such as Amazon and eBay. Besides keeping your perfectly cooked food moist, tender and hot, using a chafing dish will give your barbecue a real air of professionalism.

WHAT TO DO WITH LEFTOVERS

No one likes to throw food away, but if you're intending to keep any leftovers for future use you should take a few simple precautions:

- Any perishable food left in the open, even in the shade, for longer than two hours MUST be thrown away. Remember that this time limit drops to one hour on very hot days where the temperature is above 30°C (86°F).
- Put cold items in the fridge straight away and cool hot food as quickly as possible, but don't cover hot food with cling film until it's at room temperature. This is because the moisture that condenses on the plastic film will help bacteria breed. Instead, place hot food in a cool place under a mesh cover until it's ready for the fridge, then cover with cling film.
- Never reheat food that was defrosted before cooking or was cooked straight from the freezer.
- Never reheat food cooked from fresh more than once.
- Unused raw meat should be stored in a sealed container at the bottom of the fridge to stop drips contaminating cooked food.
- Don't overload your fridge as it won't chill items efficiently.

FEED THE FIRE

Believe it or not, the fuel you use can also be a key part of barbecue hygiene because your choice of fire will affect the measures you need to take to avoid any unpleasant consequences.

A gas-fuelled grill will eliminate many of the problems inherent in outdoor cooking because bottled propane is very easy to control. Simply light the burner and use the controls to adjust the heat to the required temperature. An equipment thermometer fitted to the cooking area will help maintain the optimum temperature whilst a food thermometer will help ensure food is cooked thoroughly (see page 41).

On the other hand, burning briquettes and natural charcoal can't be controlled like gas so things become slightly more complicated. Natural charcoal burns with a fierce heat, and though charcoal briquettes burn more gently both fuels can carbonise the outside of food before the inside begins to cook.

Serving charred and blackened food that's also raw in the middle is the most common cause of barbecue food poisoning, but it's also one of the easiest pitfalls to avoid. All you need to do is build and light your solid fuel fire properly.

Cooking with charcoal
You can't beat a traditional charcoal barbecue

In theory you should choose charcoal or briquettes according to the food you're going to cook. Experts use only natural charcoal for cooking small items that need a fast 'flash' cooking, such as prawns and scallops; a mix of charcoal and briquettes for medium items such as steaks and burgers; and briquettes alone for large items that need to be cooked more slowly, such as chicken portions.

In practice most of us will cook over a charcoal briquette fire because this fuel is readily available and easy to light, but whatever type or mix of fuel you use remember the following:

- Light the fire according to the guidelines in Chapter 4.
- Wait until the flames have died away, because the embers will not be hot enough to cook food properly until every briquette or piece of charcoal is covered with a fine, grey ash.
- Once this stage has been reached, spread the embers across the fire pan. A small garden rake with a metal head and a wooden handle cut down to size is ideal for this job. The bed of embers should be no more than 5cm (2in) thick and deeper in the middle than at the edges, as this will create the three basic cooking temperatures of low, medium and high.
- The essential element in expert charcoal grilling is to move the food around the cooking area to ensure each item cooks evenly without burning. Remember the centre of the cooking area will

be hottest and the edges coolest. Start by searing food in the centre of the grill and move it further towards the edges as the cooking time progresses (see also 'Times and temperatures' later in this chapter).

- If your grill is fitted with an adjustable height fire pan, remember to alter the setting for larger food items. The rule to remember is that large items should be cooked further away from the fire to ensure heat reaches the middle of the food before the outside begins to burn. If your grill lacks a moveable fire pan you can use rib and roasting racks to create different heights above the coals.
- Use equipment and food thermometers to monitor temperatures, and cook the food for an appropriate length of time.

WHEN IS IT DONE?
Deciding when food is done can be a problem, because different people have different ideas about what 'cooked' means. Take steak: some steak lovers like it rare whilst others insist it should be well done. The usual rules are that food will be safe to eat when the centre, or thickest part, is:

- Piping hot all the way through – this is especially important for fish and shellfish.
- Grey not pink – this rule is essential for any item made from minced meat, such as sausages and burgers; but beef and lamb steaks can be eaten rare, that is with some pink at the centre, if desired.
- Any juices that flow run clear – this rule is especially important for white meat, and the way to test if poultry or pork is cooked is to poke a skewer or fork into the thickest part of the meat; the liquid that oozes out should be completely clear, with no trace of red.

In truth few people can judge accurately if food is properly cooked by eye alone. Therefore every back garden barbecuer should always use a food thermometer to check if food that looks ready to eat is actually safe. Turn to the 'Times and temperatures' section later in this chapter for a list of minimum safe temperatures.

Cooking with gas

Quick and easy to use, gas is the ideal fuel for the back garden grill

Apart from lighting, the basic techniques behind gas grilling are identical to those of charcoal grilling, but here are some extra tips to help you make the most of your gas barbecue.

www.leisuregrow.com

USING GAS CYLINDERS

Charcoal grillers can always chop up some wooden deck chairs if they run out of fuel but gas grillers can only cook with bottled gas. Nothing kills the atmosphere of a barbecue quicker than the chef disappearing to buy more propane, so always keep a second bottle of gas in reserve.

Store spare gas outside, away from frost and direct sunlight, and if you have to change cylinders during a cooking session make sure the grill's heat controls and the cylinder's valve are both in the off position before you disconnect any pipes.

When you've finished cooking, turn off the gas cylinder before turning off the barbecue controls, to make sure any gas in the pipe is used up.

As we saw in the previous chapter, at the start of each season you should check the gas pipes for leaks by brushing soapy water over all the joints and watching for bubbles. If you find a leaky joint tighten it carefully (but avoid over-tightening) and repeat the soapy water test. If the leak persists take the equipment to a qualified gas engineer. Any perished or leaking tubes must be replaced with new ones designed for that model.

COOK ON A CLEAN GRILL

Old grease and food scraps must be cleaned away regularly otherwise gas jets will become blocked, creating an uneven flame, and your grill will begin to produce clouds of rancid, foul-smelling smoke. Unlike the 'clean' smoke described later, smoke from stale grease will give your food a very nasty taste. However, you can prevent this problem with regular burn-offs.

Before the first barbecue of the season light the gas, close the lid and turn the heat up to its highest setting for 30–45 minutes. This should burn away any unwanted grease, mould, insects and other contaminants that have gathered in the grill over the winter. Cleaning a warm grill is much easier than cleaning a cold one so immediately after the burn-off, switch off the heat, and when the grill is warm enough to touch safely give everything a good scrub.

Remove racks, grates and any other detachable devices so that you can get a wire brush and hot soapy water into all the hidden nooks and crannies. Use a pipe cleaner or garden wire to remove any stubborn cobwebs and other gunk from gas nozzles. Repeat

www.leisuregrow.com

this process regularly during the season, but you can reduce the burn-off time to 10–15 minutes.

After each cleaning, brush the racks with a thin layer of cooking oil, relight the gas and bake the oiled racks on a high heat for about 15 minutes.

Once upon a time the golden rule with gas grilling was to constantly brush racks with oil during cooking too, to prevent food sticking, but an increasing number of experts now favour the 'get a grip rule'. This states that when cooking a steak, it's only ready to turn when it lets go naturally. In other words, if steak sticks cook it longer until it comes free of its own accord. Personally I think that oiling is purely a matter of individual preference, so experiment and see what method suits your style of cooking.

Returning to the ideal cleaning regime for gas grills, the only part that should not be scrubbed clean is the griddle plate, because using scourers and detergents here will remove the carbonised material that forms the best cooking surface. A layer of carbon provides a useful non-stick surface where bacteria can't breed, but your griddle will only work in this way if it's been properly seasoned before you use it for the first time.

After each subsequent cooking session you'll need to restore the griddle surface. When the plate is warm enough to touch use a wide-bladed scraper to push any food debris into the waste tray. Spray the surface with clean water and use paper towels and the scraper to remove any fat residue. Repeat until the griddle surface is smooth and clean. Before you cook again reapply a fresh layer of cooking oil as described above.

Seasoning a new griddle

- Wash the new griddle plate with warm soapy water and a soft brush to remove any protective coating applied by the manufacturer. This is the last time soap needs to touch your griddle!
- When the metal is thoroughly clean spread a thick layer of cooking oil right across the griddle and use paper towels or a soft cloth to ensure all parts of the plate are covered evenly. The cooking oil should be light and suitable for frying at very high temperatures.
- Light the burner(s) under the griddle and turn the heat up as high as possible but leave the lid open. Keep the heat on high until wisps of smoke begin to dance across the surface of the plate.
- Turn off the heat and let the griddle cool until it's safe to touch. Use paper towels or a soft cloth to wipe away any unburned oil and create an even surface.
- Repeat this process a second, third and fourth time. Now you're ready to cook.

Tip

- You can also season a new skillet by covering the cooking surface with a light frying oil and baking it in an oven at 150°C (300°F) for three or four hours.

Cooking with Grillstream

Grillstream is a patented, smart grill system with full open bar technology and no overlaps, allowing full heat direct to the grilling surface. Specially shaped double grills stream dripping oil and fat away from the heat source and are specifically designed to stop any fats falling through onto hot coals or gas burners. Fats are channelled away for safe environmental sound disposal making this greener by producing less smoke during the cooking process.

Recently invented Grillstream Technology Barbecues help prevent flare-ups and stream the fat away, and are available in 360° charcoal grills or ready-fitted to Leisuregrow gas barbecues.

The double layer creates the Grillstream system

The Grillstream 360 fits most kettle BBQs

COOKING WITH VAPORISER BARS OR LAVA ROCK

A vaporiser bar is a metal device that fits over the burner. The food is placed on an open rack rather than ridged grill plate or flat griddle so that fat can drip on to the hot bar and vaporise, just as it does with briquettes. Lava rocks (also called volcanic rock) do the same job but sit in a basket over the gas burner. The chief difference between the two is that to avoid any stale grease smoke vaporiser bars should be scrubbed clean, whilst lava rocks should be turned dirty side down and given the burn-off treatment.

When using vaporisers or lava rocks the flares can sometimes become a little more intense than desired. Such heat can result in food becoming burnt, so many gas grillers keep a spray-gun full of clean water to hand to damp the flares down. However, this would seem to defeat the object, so I prefer to move the food to a different section of the cooking area and wait until the flare dies away.

If a flare turns into a fire and starts to spread you should cover the grill with a fire blanket and switch off the gas. In really serious cases use a fire extinguisher designed for use with gas barbecues and stand well back until you're sure the fire is out. NEVER use water – as I explained in the previous chapter, throwing water on burning fat can cause an explosion of rapidly expanding steam that will shower your guests in a scalding mixture of hot fat and boiling water. If you're in any doubt about a fire, call the fire brigade immediately.

Cooking with dual and interchangeable surfaces

Dual and interchangeable surface grills are designed to offer a choice of cooking areas, usually a flat griddle plate and a ridged grill pan. A dual surface grill will have both these areas side by side so that they can be used together. Conversely, an interchangeable grill can only accommodate one option or the other at any one time.

In truth both a griddle plate and a grill pan use indirect heat to cook the food, so using one surface or the other is often just a matter of personal taste. The ridged grill pan is supposed to cook steaks, chicken pieces and sausages better because it lifts the food above the melted fat. A flat griddle, however, is supposed to cook food that has a larger but thinner surface area better, such as burgers and sliced vegetables, because more of the food is in contact with the hot plate.

Cooking with smoke

Burning wood releases a cocktail of chemicals that have three beneficial effects: formaldehyde and acetic acid are antimicrobials that kill bacteria, phenols are antioxidants that prevent animal fat becoming rancid, and oxidised plant sugars give smoked food that characteristic caramelised flavour. Smoking has consequently been used since the dawn of time to preserve, cook and flavour food, and over the centuries two distinct methods of smoking have evolved: cold smoking and hot smoking.

Both hot and cold smoking involve heating woodchips in a metal pan placed over a heat source and keeping them smouldering so that they produce smoke without bursting into flame. Cold smoking does this by using low temperatures whilst hot smoking restricts the flow of air. These different approaches mean cold smoking doesn't cook food whereas hot smoking does.

COLD SMOKING

Cold smoking is used to preserve food – especially pork (ham and bacon), sea fish (cod, haddock, mackerel and herring) and game fish (salmon and trout) – whilst adding flavour. In cold smoking the temperature inside the smoker is kept between 10–32°C (50–90°F), which is enough to 'cure' the food without cooking it. Because cold smoking doesn't cook food this process is best left to commercial smokehouses and isn't recommended for back garden barbecuers.

HOT SMOKING

Hot smoking, however, keeps temperatures inside the smoker above 90–95°C (190–205°F) but below 120–125°C (245–260°F). Controlling temperature is important, because below the minimum temperature food doesn't cook properly but above the maximum temperature fat evaporates, making food dry and tough.

Hot smoking, if done properly, renders food safe to eat without further cooking, so this method can be used by amateur smokers, and there are several styles of back garden smoker now available for domestic use.

www.macsbbq.co.uk

OFFSET SMOKERS

An offset smoker consists of two different-sized cylinders laid horizontally on a frame. The smaller cylinder is placed slightly lower than the larger, and at the other end of the larger cylinder there's a chimney. This design makes these devices look like old steam engines being cut up for scrap, but there's method in the offset smoker's madness.

The small cylinder is the firebox for the charcoal and woodchips whilst the large cylinder is the cooking area. The chimney draws smoke and indirect heat from the firebox through the cooking chamber to both cook and flavour the food. The best models are also fitted with a shelf for food preparation, an integral equipment thermometer and wheels for ease of transport and storage.

SOLID FUEL UPRIGHT DRUM SMOKERS (UDS)

For some reason fans of this form of outdoor cooking like to insult their favourite piece of kit, so the UDS is often called the Ugly Drum Smoker. As you've probably guessed, the modern UDS evolved from primitive devices fashioned from old 44-gallon oil drums, but the two key components have hardly changed.

A UDS consists of a vertical steel cylinder with a fire pan at the bottom to hold the hot charcoal or briquettes. Above the fire pan there's another pan for woodchips, and above this there are several cooking racks. The lid and base have adjustable ventilation holes allowing the temperature inside to be controlled. The best models also have meat hooks fastened inside the top and a temperature gauge.

GAS UDS

Just as the gas grill is related to the charcoal grill, so the propane gas smoker is related to the charcoal UDS. The design of the gas smoker is identical to the solid fuel variety and the only difference is that the fuel is bottled propane. The burning gas heats woodchips in the fire pan to create both the smoke and heat needed to cook the food.

The gas UDS is only ventilated at the top – this reduces the amount of oxygen inside the cylinder and this prevents the wood from catching fire. Unlike the solid fuel UDS the temperature is controlled by regulating the supply of gas through an easily adjustable valve at the base of the drum.

VERTICAL WATER SMOKERS

This seemingly contradictory device is a variation on the gas or solid fuel UDS. The water smoker places a pan of water between the woodchips and the food being smoked. The theory is that the water creates humidity that helps maintain a constant temperature and keeps the food moist. Critics point out that the water pan eliminates the little flash fires caused by fat dripping on to the hot coals, and this flaw produces a less authentic barbecue flavour.

ELECTRIC SMOKERS

These devices, which can be the size of a fridge freezer, are really only suited to those planning on building their own smoke house, but for those that can afford it these high-tech devices feature automatic hoppers that keep the woodchip pan topped up. All you have to do is fill the racks with food, turn on, and wait.

www.macsbbq.co.uk

www.macsbbq.co.uk

Whatever type of smoker you choose, remember that they all take a lot longer to cook food than a standard gas or charcoal grill, so be prepared to wait several hours before your smoked ribs are ready. However, if you want to give food a smoky flavour quickly you can always use a smoker box placed on your gas or charcoal barbecue.

SMOKER BOXES AND SMOKER POTS

Of course, charcoal grillers can simply sprinkle handfuls of aromatic woodchips directly on to glowing embers to produce sweet-smelling smoke, but even damp wood will quickly catch fire if scattered on hot coals.

Equally, spreading sawdust on a gas grill is downright dangerous, so to help wood smoulder safely and for longer both charcoal and gas grillers should use a proper smoker box.

Rectangular smoker boxes and cylindrical smoker pots are a halfway house between hot and cold smoking. In other words, they offer a way of adding a smoky flavour to meat, fish and vegetables whilst the heat from the burning charcoal, briquettes or gas actually cooks the food.

A good smoker box should last for years and their cast iron or stainless steel construction will ensure woodchips smoulder evenly, but you can also make your own. Just fill a disposable aluminium roasting tin with soaked woodchips to a depth of about 50mm (2in), cover the tray with aluminium foil and pierce this lid with large holes to let the smoke out.

These throwaway smoker boxes are ideal for experimenting with different woodchips and honing your smoking technique.

HOW TO USE A SMOKER BOX

CHARCOAL/BRIQUETTE GRILLS

Soak the woodchips in clean, cold water for a minimum of 30 minutes and ideally for about an hour. To stop the wood from floating on the surface, use two old saucepans of concentric sizes. Put the woodchips in the bottom of the larger pan, add water, then place the smaller pan on top. Fill the smaller pan with water to weigh it down – this will keep the woodchips on the bottom of the larger pan. Keep a bucket handy to drain the water when the chips are ready. You can use this water later for cooling hot racks and other tasks.

Next pile the unlit charcoal or briquettes around the smoker box and light as normal. If you're using a charcoal starter soak the woodchips while you're heating up the charcoal, then place the box with the damp woodchips in the centre of the cold fire pan, add the hot charcoal, and use your rake or tongs to pile the heated coals around it.

Once the woodchips start to smoulder and smoke place the food on the grill, and if your barbecue has a lid adjust the ventilators to ensure smoke circulates freely. If you smoke food in an unventilated grill it will absorb the foul tasting by-products produced by burning. You can also open and close the lid to regulate how much the food is exposed to the smoke, thus creating different intensities of flavour.

GAS GRILLS

Soak the woodchips in water as before and place them in the smoker box. Before you light/preheat the barbecue, remove the grill rack and place the smoker box over the burner. The box should sit clear of the gas jets below and the grill rack above; often the best place for it is on the vaporiser bars (if fitted).

After replacing the grill rack turn on the heat and close the lid for the cooking area to preheat. When the chips begin to smoke the grill is ready and you can place the food inside. Again, if your gas grill has a lid use it to regulate the amount of exposure the food has to the smoke.

COOKING WITH HICKORY AND OTHER WOODCHIPS OR PELLETS

Besides a smoker box, the other essential ingredient in smoking food is the woodchips, but you can't use just any wood. Pine and other softwoods contain high levels of resin, which turns to bitter-tasting creosote when burned. Instead you need non-resinous hardwoods. In Britain and Europe oak, alder or apple are the traditional woods for smoking, but an increasing number of modern barbecuers favour American hickory.

HICKORY

There are 19 species of hickory tree native to the south-eastern states of the USA, and once upon a time frontiersmen used hickory-handled axes to chop hickory logs for their campfires. Thus hickory became an important ingredient in the distinctive taste of Southern Style barbecue.

Nowadays pre-packed bags of chipped hickory are readily available from good garden centres, supermarkets and DIY stores. If you still can't find hickory wood the taste can be replicated by using hickory-flavoured marinades and rubs, but nothing beats the real thing.

MESQUITE

Hickory trees become less common west of the Mississippi, so Texan, Arizonan and Californian barbecuers traditionally use wood from the mesquite tree, a thorny, drought-resistant plant which thrives in arid and semi-desert conditions.

Where water is abundant mesquite can grow to a height of 9m (30ft), but if water is scarce it will rarely grow higher than the surrounding shrubs. There are several species including screw-bean, velvet and honey, whose flowers are favourites of bees. Mesquite honey has a nutty taste, as does the flour made from the tree's dried seedpods.

Ranchers regard mesquite, also called Texas ironwood (because it's so hard to cut), as a troublesome weed, which is perhaps why they started burning mesquite wood on their campfires. Luckily for hungry cowboys mesquite makes fantastic firewood as it burns slowly with a lot of heat.

For barbecuers wanting to recreate the Texas brand of Southern barbecue a smoker box of mesquite wood is a must. You can use it to add its characteristic nut flavour to steaks, chicken, pork, fish and vegetables.

OTHER WOODS

Besides hickory and mesquite most barbecue supply stores now sell a range of woodchips for smoker boxes. Oak, apple and beech remain popular, and with a little experimentation you can blend different woods to create your own special recipe.

PELLETS

Wood pellets are used in smoker boxes on some specially-made grills but can be used in most other barbecues with a smoke pot. Natural wood is compacted into small pellets, giving more heat and flavour for their volume. Many are made from waste wood fibre and they're available in many 'flavours'.

Tips for cooking with woodchips

- Smoking can add a distinct pink circle around the inner edge of smoked meats, called the smoke ring, which makes it difficult to tell if food is completely cooked. Novice smokers should therefore use a food thermometer to check that everything is thoroughly cooked.
- Even pre-soaked woodchips will burn away after around 15 minutes in a hot smoke box, so check the supply every quarter of an hour.
- If you have just one sort of wood available you can vary the flavour by soaking the woodchips in apple juice, wine, brandy, whisky or any other liquid, but don't use your best 25-year-old single malt unless you want to treat your guests to something really special.
- Remember to use gloves and tongs when handling hot coals, racks and smoker boxes. Though wood smoke has anti-bacterial and preservative properties it's of no help in treating burns!

Times and temperatures

No two grills, even if they're identical models, will cook food at the same temperature, and each different combination of grilling method, fuel and even the weather will also affect cooking times. Therefore any times or temperatures given in a recipe must ALWAYS be regarded as approximate, and you must rely on your own judgement and/or a food thermometer to ensure that food is cooked properly.

The following charts are no exception, but they should at least give you a rough idea of the minimum times and temperatures at which different foods should be cooked.

GAS AND CHARCOAL

Gas grillers can simply set their controls to the high, medium and low temperatures indicated, but charcoal grillers need to arrange their hot charcoal properly (slightly deeper at the centre than the edges) so that their grill also has these three cooking zones.

Once you've established the correct heat levels simply place each item of food in the appropriate part of the grill as indicated by the chart.

If you're cooking a variety of items in the high–medium category start with the food that requires the longest cooking time and place each item on the hot area at the centre of the grill. When all the sides have been seared (see below), move the food away from the centre to the medium area for the rest of its cooking period. Now place more items in the vacant central hot spot and repeat the process as necessary.

During cooking turn each item regularly to ensure the heat is applied evenly to all parts. If food begins to char towards the end of its cooking time move it towards the edge or turn down the heat.

Once the cooking time has elapsed remove a sample item from the heat and check it's done. Cut the item in half to check by eye AND use a food thermometer such as a Thermapen to confirm that the food is at the minimum safe serving temperature shown by the chart. To repeat, the temperatures given are approximate, and if you're in any doubt at all cook the item for a little longer.

Note that these cooking times are based on the approximate thickness of different items (steaks, sausages and chops = 25mm/1in thick, burgers = 20mm/¾in thick). Larger items will require longer cooking times than those indicated.

They're also based on cooking the items from fresh. Frozen food must be defrosted thoroughly before cooking on a barbecue.

Key		
Heat	Charcoal/briquette grill placement	Approximate gas grill settings
High	Centre	Above 285°C (550°F)
Medium	Inner area	230–260°C (450–500°F)
Low	Outer edge	150–200°C (300–400°F)

Beef			
	Cooking area temperature	Cooking time	Approx internal temperature
Steaks – rare	High	6–8 minutes	Over 65°C (145°F)
Steaks – medium	High	10–15 minutes	Over 70°C (160°F)
Steaks – well done	High–medium	15–20 minutes	Over 75°C (170°F)
Burgers – rare	High–medium	6–8 minutes	Over 70°C (160°F)
Burgers – medium	High–medium	9–10 minutes	Over 70°C (160°F)
Burgers – well done	High–medium	12–15 minutes	Over 75°C (170°F)
Kebabs – rare	High	6–8 minutes	Over 70°C (160°F)
Kebabs – medium	High	10–15 minutes	Over 70°C (160°F)
Kebabs – well done	High	15–20 minutes	Over 75°C (170°F)

Lamb

	Cooking area temperature	Cooking time	Approx internal temperature
Chops – rare	High–medium	8–10 minutes	Over 65°C (145°F)
Chops – medium	High–medium	12–15 minutes	Over 70°C (160°F)
Chops – well done	High–medium	18–20 minutes	Over 75°C (170°F)
Burgers – rare	High–medium	6–8 minutes	Over 70°C (160°F)
Burgers – medium	High–medium	9–11 minutes	Over 70°C (160°F)
Burgers – well done	High–medium	12–15 minutes	Over 75°C (170°F)
Steaks – rare	High–medium	5–7 minutes	Over 65°C (145°F)
Steaks – medium	High–medium	8–10 minutes	Over 70°C (160°F)
Steaks – well done	Medium–high	14–18 minutes	Over 75°C (170°F)
Kebabs – rare	High	6–8 minutes	Over 70°C (160°F)
Kebabs – medium	High	9–11 minutes	Over 70°C (160°F)
Kebabs – well done	High	12–15 minutes	Over 75°C (170°F)

Poultry

	Cooking area temperature	Cooking time	Approx internal temperature
Chicken breast – boneless	High–medium	18–22 minutes	Over 80°C (180°F)
Chicken breast – bone in	High–medium	25–30 minutes	Over 80°C (180°F)
Chicken drumsticks	High–medium	25–30 minutes	Over 80°C (180°F)
Chicken burgers	High–medium	15–18 minutes	Over 75°C (165°F)
Chicken kebabs	High–medium	13–15 minutes	Over 75°C (165°F)
Duck breast – boneless	High–medium	15–20 minutes	Over 80°C (180°F)
Duck half	High–medium	35–40 minutes	Over 80°C (180°F)

Pork

	Cooking area temperature	Cooking time	Approx internal temperature
Steaks/ chops	High–medium	18–20 minutes	Over 70°C (160°F)
Burgers	Medium	15–18 minutes	Over 70°C (160°F)
Sausages (thick)	High–medium	8–12 minutes	Over 70°C (160°F)
Spare ribs	High–medium	30–40 minutes	Over 70°C (160°F)
Kebabs	High–medium	13–15 minutes	Over 70°C (160°F)

Fish

	Cooking area temperature	Cooking time	Approx internal temperature
Salmon and trout (whole, 0.9–2.2kg / 2–5lb)	High–medium	10–20 minutes	Over 65°C (145°F)
Salmon and tuna steaks	High–medium	9–10 minutes	Over 65°C (145°F)
King prawns – in shell	Low	6–8 minutes	Over 65°C (145°F)
King prawns – shelled	High–medium	4–5 minutes	Over 65°C (145°F)

Fruit and vegetables

	Cooking area temperature	Cooking time	Approx internal temperature
Halves	Medium–low	5–10 minutes	Over 65°C (145°F)
Pieces (in foil)	Medium–low	7–10 minutes	Over 65°C (145°F)
Slices	Medium–low	3–5 minutes	Over 65°C (145°F)
Kebabs	Medium–low	5–8 minutes	Over 65°C (145°F)
Corn on the cob	Medium	8–10 minutes	Over 65°C (145°F)

SMOKED FOOD

Judging when smoked food is ready for eating is even more difficult than with gas and charcoal grills. The chart below gives rough cooking times, but again you must use a food thermometer to check that food has reached the minimum internal temperature.

	Approximate smoking temperature	Approximate smoking time	Approx internal temperature
Beef (sliced)	100–110°C (225°F)	1½ hours per pound	80°C (180°F)
Beef (shredded)	100–110°C (225°F)	1½ hours per pound	90°C (195°F)
Pork (sliced)	100–110°C (225°F)	1½ hours per pound	80°C (180°F)
Pork (shredded)	100–110°C (225°F)	1½ hours per pound	90°C (190–200°F)
Chicken (whole)	120–125°C (250°F)	4 hours	80°C (180°F)
Chicken (legs)	120–125°C (250°F)	1½ hours	80°C (180°F)
Chicken (quarters)	120–125°C (250°F)	3 hours	80°C (180°F)
Turkey (whole)	115–120°C (240°F)	6½ hours	75°C (165°F)
Turkey (leg)	120–125°C (250°F)	4 hours	75°C (165°F)
Sausages	110–115°C (230°F)	3 hours	70°C (160°F)
Salamis	110–115°C (230°F)	2½ hours	70°C (160°F)
Spare ribs	100–120°C (225–240°F)	6 hours	80°C (180°F)
Fish up to 0.4kg (1lb)	90–95°C (190–205°F)	1½–2 hours	60°C (140°F)
Fish 0.4–0.9kg (1–2lb)	120–125°C (250°F)	2–2½ hours	60°C (140°F)
Fish 1.3–1.8kg (3–4lb)	120–125°C (250°F)	2½–3 hours	60°C (140°F)
Corn on the cob	100–110°C (225°F)	1½–2 hours	Not applicable
Potatoes	100–110°C (225°F)	2–2½ hours	Not applicable

Top tips!

- Barbecues have a wicked sense of humour and the window during which food will be at its best is always quite small. In other words, never leave food unattended on the grill, or you'll come back to burned burgers, blackened bangers and carbonised kebabs!
- If your barbecue has a lid, open and close it to regulate the heat, but use an equipment thermometer to check that the temperatures in different parts of the cooking area remain constant.
- Baste food regularly with natural juices or a marinade to preserve their moisture, but remember to use a separate bowl of marinade to the one you used for raw food.
- Beef and lamb steaks and chops will benefit from being allowed to rest for three to five minutes before serving, as this allows the internal temperature to rise, killing more bacteria and tenderising the meat. Resting items should be covered loosely with foil and kept on a ridged carving board to allow excess juice to drain away.
- Sugar burns at 130°C (265°F), so if you're using sauces or rubs that contain sugar you'll need to keep your cooking area below this temperature or the food will blacken and burn.
- When using a food thermometer to test food cooked on the bone make sure the probe doesn't touch the bone, as this will give an inaccurate reading.

Preparation

Let's be honest. At one time or another we've all smiled dutifully and lavished praise on the barbecue chef whilst trying to chew our way through a piece of bland, blackened gristle that's lost any vestige of taste.

The sad fact is that most barbecue food becomes dry, tasteless and inedible for one of three reasons: poor ingredients, poor cooking or poor preparation.

The formula for fantastic barbecue food works like this: the worse the ingredients or the cooking, the more important preparation becomes.

Still not convinced? Let me put it another way. Some foods, such as the finest Aberdeen Angus steaks, need nothing more than a little light seasoning and cooking at the right temperatures to taste delicious, but cheaper cuts of meat will always benefit from some form of preparation.

Cheap chicken – that most tasteless of barbecue food – can be transformed by soaking in a mouth-watering marinade. 'Super Saver' steaks can taste like the finest sirloins if rubbed with a dry mix or paste full of herbs and spices, and even the humble sausage can become a taste sensation if grilled alongside herb brushes.

To put it bluntly, a barbecue doesn't lend itself to cooking subtle cuisine; in fact great grilling is all about intense flavours and intense seasoning. Food that's been marinated takes on a wonderful flavour and is less likely to dry out, so proper preparation is as essential to great barbecuing as a good grill and proper tools.

However, before we embark on our journey through the fascinating world of marinades, rubs, glazes and brushes, let's start with the simplest form of preparation – searing.

SEARING

The short application of a very hot heat to the surface of food is called searing, and it achieves two things. It seals in natural juices, keeping food moist, and caramelises the surface of food, creating a crisp, almost charred edge full of natural flavour.

Searing any cut of beef, lamb or pork couldn't be easier. For charcoal grills, place the meat in the centre of the cooking area; for gas grills, turn up the gas to high and leave the food for one minute before turning. Leave for a further minute, then turn the gas down, or move the food to a cooler part of a charcoal grill, for the rest of the cooking time.

MARINADES

Searing works best with good cuts of meat but marinades will work with anything. In fact I'd go so far as to say that marinades are the most important weapon in the war to convince people that barbecuing is the best form of cooking ever invented!

A good marinade not only flavours food, it helps keep it moist and tender during cooking. At its most basic level a marinade is just a mixture of herbs and spices held together by a binding agent, and most fall into one of two categories:

■ Acidic marinades, based on wine, vinegar, mustard, soy sauce or citrus fruit juices that help tenderise the meat.
■ Oil and paste marinades, which form a crust whilst cooking to seal in the juices that help tenderise the meat.

Of course, the secret is finding the right blend of herbs and spices to complement the food being cooked, and there are plenty of suggestions in the recipe section later in this book. In the meantime here are some dos and don'ts relating to marinades.

MARINATING TIMES

Marinating for the correct length of time is crucial to bringing out the distinct flavours of different foods, but these times vary according to the size and type of food you want to flavour. As general rule you should allow one cup (250ml) of marinade for every half-kilo (1lb) of meat and marinate for the following times:

Food	Approximate marinating times
Fish	1 to 2 hours
Shellfish	30 minutes to 1 hour
Chicken (whole)	4 to 6 hours
Chicken (pieces)	2 to 6 hours
Turkey (whole)	Overnight (inside the fridge)
Turkey (pieces)	4 to 8 hours
Pork	3 to 4 hours
Red meat	Overnight (inside the fridge)
Kebabs	4 to 6 hours
Spare ribs	6 to 8 hours
Vegetables	1 to 2½ hours

Besides marinating for the correct length of time, make sure that:

- The marinade is applied evenly to all parts of the food. If the dish is too shallow to allow the liquid to cover the food, turn the food halfway through the marinating period.
- You want the marinade to cling to the meat, but don't make the mix too thick or it won't penetrate properly.
- Score the skin to allow the marinade to penetrate fully, but don't prick or puncture the flesh beneath as this will let the marinade leak out!
- Always use glass, ceramic or plastic containers for marinating because metal vessels will react with the ingredients.
- Any container used for marinating should have a lid to keep the goodness in and the air, dust, flies and other contaminants out. Large plastic ice cream tubs, thoroughly washed and dried, are ideal.
- During cooking reapply the marinade so that the food holds the flavour in the heat. But never reapply marinade used for raw meat on to cooked or cooking food. Instead keep two bowls, one for cooking and one for raw food.
- If marinating for more than one hour place the food in the refrigerator.
- Don't marinate delicate meats like fish or poultry for too long or the acid in the liquid will start to 'digest' the flesh!
- Use fresh herbs wherever possible. If you have to use dried herbs crush them first to release the oils.
- Zipped plastic pouches are great for marinating as you can 'squish' them to mix everything together.

- Discard any unused marinade and never serve used marinade as a sauce. Instead, keep a quantity in reserve and boil for two to three minutes before serving.

INJECTING MARINADES

If you don't have the time to marinate for several hours, you can inject the meat with marinade using a syringe designed for the job. The marinade must be quite thin to squeeze through the needle, and for a real short cut you can use a ready-made condiment such as soy sauce, Worcester sauce or even wine and fruit juices.

Different meats will absorb different amounts of marinade, so some experimentation is required, but as a rough guide 30–60ml (1–2fl oz) per half-kilo or pound of meat should be enough.

To use an injector, pour some olive oil over the rubber parts of the plunger before attaching the needle. Pour the marinade into a clean container to prevent cross-contamination and fill the injector as you would any syringe.

Place the injector into the meat at an angle of 45° and slowly depress the plunger as you pull the injector out. Space each application evenly but allow for different thicknesses of meat. For example, with a whole chicken inject equal amounts into each drumstick and thigh, but double the amount for each breast.

Top tip!

Use a finely ground rub on thinner cuts and a coarser powder on thicker cuts of meat.

RUBS

A barbecue rub is simply a mix of ground herbs and spices rubbed into meat to enhance its flavour, but the vital extra ingredient that turns simple seasoning into a rub is sugar. During cooking the sugar caramelises, forming a crust that seals in the juices and creates the sweet flavours that are so characteristic of American-style barbecued food.

As with marinades, rubs can be used wet (mixed with a binding agent into a paste) or dry (as a powder), but the crucial difference is that rubs are applied immediately before cooking. This makes rubs quicker and easier to use than marinades, and they're especially useful for campfires and other barbecues where long hours of marinating in huge vats of liquid are impossible.

That said, it's a good idea to let the meat rest for as long as you can after applying the rub so that the herbs and spices have a chance to penetrate. If you have the time the marinating chart can also be applied to rubs.

There are numerous ready-made rubs on the market so it makes sense to keep a jar or two of your favourites in the cupboard, just in case the sun suddenly breaks through on a grey day. Of course, if you have the time you can also make your own and there are some ideas for wet and dry rubs in the recipe section.

To apply the rub, sprinkle the powder or spread the paste over the food smoothly and evenly. Use your fingertips or the back of a tablespoon to gently massage the herbs and spices into the meat. With dry rubs, a light brushing of olive oil or mustard will help the powder stick. If you reapply a rub during cooking remember to use different pots of rub for raw and cooking food, and also a clean spoon.

SAUCES AND GLAZES

Technically a sauce should only be applied after cooking has finished, but as some people like to brush food with a little zingy barbecue sauce whilst it's cooking, to create a glaze, I'll give it a mention here.

A glaze is different to a rub or a marinade because it only flavours the surface of the meat rather than being absorbed throughout. Again, it's a quick and easy flavour enhancer.

To create a glaze, brush the sauce on to the food towards the end of the cooking process. Don't apply too early or it'll burn; equally, don't leave it too late or there won't be enough time for the sugar to caramelise. To recreate the high gloss shine that's such a distinctive feature of Chinese barbecued spare ribs, stir some honey into the sauce before brushing it on. As before you must keep any sauce, containers and utensils used during cooking separate from any sauce served after cooking has finished.

In America's 'Barbecue Belt' the nature of the local barbecue sauce has become an important symbol of individual statehood. Here are the best-known regional variants:

Sauce	Home state
Thick tomato – sweet, spicy and mildly hot.	Missouri (Kansas City)
Thin tomato with molasses and Worcestershire sauce.	Texas
Thin tomato with lemon, lime, vinegar and butter.	Florida
Thin mustard with tomato and vinegar.	South Carolina (south) and Georgia
Thin vinegar with sugar, salt, crushed red pepper and black peppercorns.	North Carolina (east)
Black vinegar with Worcestershire sauce.	Kentucky
Sweet and sour with pineapple fruit and juice.	Hawaii
Soy sauce with peanuts and mild chillies.	California (Chinese communities)

HERB BRUSHES

Let's assume the dog has eaten all your lovely Lincolnshire sausages; your guests are expecting to be served beautiful herby bangers, but all you have left is a packet of economy chipolatas with about as much taste as a 1970s interior designer.

Don't despair, because a brush made from sprigs of dried herbs tied together will transform any insipid food into a taste sensation.

To make a herb brush simply use heatproof cooking twine to tie bunches of fresh or dried herbs together. You can mix and match different herbs depending on your taste and the contents of your kitchen cupboard or garden, but plants with woody stems such as thyme, rosemary and sage work best.

You can lay the herb brush on or next to the food as it cooks and close the grill lid so that the food absorbs more of the aroma. Alternatively you can use the brush to baste the meat so that all the flavours mingle with the meat juices. If you use the basting method, tying the herb brush to the blunt end of a wooden spoon will be a help.

MOPS

A mop is 'basting plus' – in other words herbs and spices are added to the meat juices before being spooned over the meat. You can add just about anything to melted fat to create a mop – fruit juice, stock, vinegar, Worcestershire sauce, boiled marinades and even beer are all very popular.

Mops containing meat juices should be applied hot, so heat the mix to boiling point for a few minutes then keep the pan simmering

Average weight of each fillet (cleaned and boned)	Approx soaking time (if skin is left on add 25% more time)
Under 0.1kg (¼lb)	30 minutes
0.1–0.2kg (¼–½lb)	45 minutes
0.2–0.5kg (½–1lb)	1 hour
0.5–0.9kg (1–2lb)	2 hours
0.9–1.3kg (2–3lb)	3 hours
1.3–1.8kg (3–4lb)	4 hours
1.8–2.7kg (4–6lb)	5 hours
2.7–4.5kg (6–10lb)	24 hours

by placing it at the side of the cooking area away from the fiercest heat. Boiling and simmering should help blend the ingredients and kill any food-poisoning bugs, but remember to stir the mop pan regularly to prevent burning.

Mops should be used in conjunction with a complementary rub and should be applied during the second half of the food's cooking time. This will allow the rub to form the necessary crust first. Also, every time you lift the lid of your grill or smoker to add the mop you lower the interior temperature and increase the cooking time, so use a basting brush or misting spray to apply the mop no more than every 30 minutes for small items and every 45 minutes for larger food.

BRINING

The word 'marinade' is actually derived from the Latin marinara, meaning 'from the sea', which is a clue to the fact that the first marinade was actually salty seawater. Brine is simply man-made salt water and brining is a method of pre-soaking food, especially fish and poultry, in brine to keep it moist during cooking. Brining is a particularly useful preparation for smoking.

The theory behind brining is that a natural process called osmosis causes the water in the brine to flow deep into the fibres of the meat. Food soaked in brine can therefore gain as much as 20% in weight, and this 'super soaking' should help the food stay moist during cooking. As an added bonus, osmosis also draws into the meat any flavouring added to the salt water, such as Tabasco or Worcestershire sauce, to add even more flavour.

Brine is made by adding roughly 350ml (1½ cups) of sea salt to 4.5 litres (one gallon) of tap water. The salt must be iodine free, and if your tap water is chlorinated it's a good idea to filter it first.

Pour the water into a large plastic or ceramic dish (not metal, because even stainless steel will react with the salt) and stir in the salt with a wooden or plastic spoon. Leave the lid off to let any chlorine released by the salt disperse. At this point you can also add any seasoning, such as white wine, peppercorns, dill or garlic according to taste.

Clean the fish or meat and place the pieces in the dish. Now leave to soak according to the chart below – but remember that the time is governed by the size of the pieces of food, not by the total weight of the food being soaked.

If you're brining before smoking, when the soaking has finished rinse and place the fish or meat on oiled racks inside the cold smoker to dry. Open the vents to ensure a good circulation of air. The food should dry for about an hour or until a thin, natural glaze, called the pellicle, has formed. Remove the food before lighting the smoker; when the internal temperature has reached the required heat return the food to the smoker to cook.

CHAPTER 6
ALTERNATIVE OUTDOOR COOKING

A GUIDE TO CHIMENEAS, BACK GARDEN OVENS, SOUTHERN BARBECUE PITS AND SPIT ROASTS

Besides grilling and smoking, you can also bake and roast food outdoors; but, with the exception of pot and spit roasting, to do this you'll need a back garden oven. Generally speaking all outdoor ovens fall into one of three categories:

- Free-standing ovens such as chimeneas.
- Permanent ovens such as brick/masonry bread and pizza ovens.
- Earth ovens such as the Hawaiian luau.

These devices are almost always wood-fired, meaning they take much longer to prepare than gas or charcoal barbecues, but if you have the time there's nothing more satisfying than baking your own bread or roasting mouth-watering meat in your own outdoor oven. You can also use your oven in conjunction with an ordinary gas or charcoal grill to cook a truly memorable barbecue banquet!

As you've probably realised, a permanent outdoor oven will take up a lot of your spare time, money and garden space, so let's start with the free-standing versions such as chimeneas. These are much cheaper than the permanent brick varieties and are therefore an ideal way to begin outdoor baking and roasting.

A wood-fired oven – the perfect way to cook pizzas

Cooking with free-standing ovens
Large plant pot, patio-heater or outdoor oven? Just what is a chimenea good for?

In recent years the chimenea (or chiminea) has become a popular addition to many British and American gardens, but this unique form of barbecue oven is actually Mexican in origin.

Long ago, Spanish conquistadors exploring the highlands of southern Mexico discovered the native peoples using bottle-shaped, wood-burning ovens for both cooking and heating. The ingenious design was so perfectly adapted to these functions that the chimenea quickly became a feature of colonial haciendas across Mexico and the south-west USA.

As the name suggests, the secret of the chimenea is its chimney. The addition of a flue to a spherical fire bowl and cooking chamber creates a powerful draft that burns wood with exceptional efficiency. Even the poorest Mexican peon could feed and warm his family with a few sticks of pinyon wood in a chimenea, and as an added bonus the smoke from the chimney kept mosquitoes and flies away.

The ability to heat, cook and repel insects has made this form of front-loading, free-standing outdoor oven/fireplace highly popular from Los Angeles to Leicester and Houston to Hartlepool, but the true chimenea should not be confused with brazier-style patio heaters. There are plenty of simple fire baskets on the market but only a chimenea will feed as well as warm your guests.

CHOOSING A CHIMENEA

The first chimeneas to appear in the UK were ceramic, but harder-wearing cast iron, steel and even aluminium versions are now becoming increasingly popular. Both materials perform the chimenea's cooking and heating functions equally well, but there are some advantages and disadvantages with each that may sway your decision when it comes to buying one:

It may sound obvious, but whatever style or design you choose make sure your chimenea is actually designed for burning combustible material. There are things on the market that look like chimeneas but which are little better than large plant pots. These 'faux' chimeneas can shatter the moment you light a fire, so try and buy the best model you can afford.

A good outdoor chimenea will have a heatproof stand, usually a tripod made of hard-wearing cast iron; a rain lid to prevent the fire bowl from filling with rainwater; and a large mouth at the front of the fire bowl for easy lighting and cooking. Traditional chimenea designs don't have doors, whilst the best modern models have grates, cooking racks, mesh spark guards and other extras. These can be very useful if you want to cook with a chimenea.

Material	Advantages	Disadvantages
Metal (cast iron, steel or aluminium)	Long-lasting. Weatherproof. Won't chip or crack in normal use. Doesn't require sealing or seasoning before use.	Expensive. Heavy and difficult to move. Some self-assembly usually required. Requires regular painting and oiling. Prone to rust unless properly maintained.
Ceramic (clay or terracotta)	More authentic. Cheaper than metal varieties. Lighter and easier to move than cast iron. No complex assembly required.	Not weatherproof unless sealed. Prone to cracking unless properly maintained. Exterior requires sealing before use and at least once a year thereafter. Interior requires seasoning before use.

www.garden4less.co.uk

One especially useful feature fitted to more expensive cast iron models is a grill rack on a pivot that can be swung out of the fire bowl. This allows you to check and turn food without having to rummage around inside the inferno. With cheaper clay chimeneas without racks fitted you can use grid irons, skewers and simple foil parcels placed directly on the embers to cook food.

SITING A CHIMENEA

Once you've got your chimenea home, the rules for positioning it are identical to those for any other type of barbecue. You should choose a firm, flat, stable surface at least 7.5m (25ft) from any building, fence or other structure and well away from any overhanging awnings, trees or anything else that might be ignited by a rogue spark.

Patios and terraces made of flagstones or gravel are ideal sites for a *chimenea* but wooden decking is not, unless you place it on a fireproof pad large enough to catch any embers that may spill from the fire bowl.

www.garden4less.co.uk

SEALING, SEASONING AND INSULATING A CLAY CHIMENEA

In Old Mexico cracked fire bowls were easily repaired with mud from the nearest riverbank, but in a cold, wet environment cracking is one of the biggest problems facing clay chimeneas. However, though a winter of rain, snow and frost followed by a summer of intense heat from cooking fires will soon shatter a clay chimenea, you can reduce the risk with proper preparation.

www.garden4less.co.uk

Before cooking with your clay chimenea for the first time use a soft decorators' paintbrush to apply a recommended sealant over the entire exterior. This will fill microscopic pores and hairline cracks, making the clay weatherproof. If water can't penetrate the clay, it can't open a crack by expanding and contracting in hot and cold conditions. After the initial treatment, reapply the sealant at least once a year at the end of each season.

After the exterior sealant has dried you should season the interior with a series of five to ten small fires made from twigs and sticks. Allow each fire to burn out and wait for the chimenea to cool before lighting the next fire, which should be slightly larger than the previous one. These fires will help prevent cracking by gently hardening and preparing the interior of the fire bowl for the intense heat needed for cooking.

Most chimeneas are now supplied with a grating to hold the burning fuel away from the surface of the fire bowl, but if you've bought a ceramic chimenea without such a fire grate you should insulate the bowl to protect the brittle clay from the direct heat of burning wood.

To do this, fill the bowl with pea gravel or sand – children's sandpit sand is ideal – to a depth of 7–10cm (3–4in) below the mouth. Then place two house bricks about 15cm (6in) apart on top. The bricks will create a hotter fire because they'll act as fire dogs that keep burning wood above the ash and allow air to circulate.

PREPARING A METAL CHIMENEA

Cast iron or steel chimeneas don't need seasoning like clay varieties but you should check that the exterior has been painted with a proper heatproof paint designed for outdoor use.

The better models will have the necessary weatherproofing applied by the manufacturer, but with cheaper models the paintwork can be very thin. If the paintwork looks poor you should consider applying an extra coat or two to prevent rust spots appearing after the first shower of rain. Suitable heat-resistant exterior metal paint, in handy spray cans, is readily available from DIY stores.

LIGHTING A FIRE IN A CHIMENEA

We've all tried to light damp or green wood that hasn't been properly seasoned and still been surprised when the logs smoulder weakly for a few minutes before going out. But I'm afraid there's no alternative – unless your firewood is dry and well seasoned you're simply wasting matches, so keep your logs and kindling under cover and light any fire in a chimenea using the pyramid method:

- Scrunch some newspaper into balls and arrange small twigs in a cone around this core.
- Add a layer of larger sticks, then light the newspaper using a long splint made of twisted paper.
- Add larger sticks until you have a bed of embers glowing red hot.
- Once you have enough embers you're ready for the logs, which should be no more than 30cm (1ft) long and 10cm (4in) thick. Lay these on the embers or across the bricks/fire dogs (if fitted) and repeat as necessary.
- If flames start to appear at the top of the chimney the fire is too fierce, and you need to let it burn down before adding more fuel.

www.garden4less.co.uk

 No firelighters or lighter fuel

WARNING! Never light a chimenea's fire with firelighters or lighter fuel, even if it's recommended for barbecues. Burning these chemicals in a confined space can result in the chimenea exploding. At the very least the interior will become coated with unburned chemicals and your food will taste of paraffin for months.

WHAT TO BURN

If you're using your chimenea for heating alone then any wood can be burned. But if you want to cook with it there are a few sensible rules to follow.

Personally I'd avoid burning softwood on an enclosed cooking fire because the resin in pine burns with an acrid, sooty flame that gives food a bitter taste. Neither would I use pellets designed for indoor solid fuel stoves, as these burn too hot, especially for clay chimeneas.

I'd also avoid any briquette-style 'easy-lighting' logs when cooking on a chimenea, because these are usually made from sawdust and the chemicals in the binding agent can taint food. Finally I'd never use any wood that's been pressure-treated, painted, stained or varnished, as the chemicals released when paints or preservatives are burned are very toxic.

As with smokers, the best wood for chimenea cooking is well-seasoned hardwood. Mexican pinyon wood is perfect, if you can get it. Hickory and mesquite, the traditional American barbecue woods, are also ideal, but be careful because these logs can burn fiercely, and too much heat will crack the fire bowl even after careful sealing and seasoning.

If you can't find these exotic timbers, European hardwoods such as beech or apple are best. Oak can be used, but oak logs are expensive and can be very difficult to light because the grain is so dense.

As a general rule natural charcoal and charcoal briquettes burn too hot for clay chimeneas but can be used in metal varieties. However, using these fuels cancels the advantages that using a chimenea has over ordinary charcoal grills (see below). In any case, proper chimeneas are designed to burn logs, so if you want to use charcoal you will probably need a fire grate with a finer mesh than the one supplied, otherwise the pieces will fall through the holes!

COOKING ON A CHIMENEA

Many chimeneas, both cast iron and ceramic, now come with a removable top so that the fire bowl can be used for cooking like an ordinary barbecue, but again this seems to defeat the whole point of buying a chimenea!

The chimenea's unique selling point is that it's a hybrid device that combines all the best qualities of an oven, grill and smoker. Like a grill, the chimenea cooks food by using direct heat from the hot embers, but unlike a grill, which only cooks from below, the bottle shape of the chimenea acts as an oven, so that food is cooked from both above and below. The design of the chimenea also helps

keep meat moist and tender during cooking, and because the fuel used is – or should be – wood everything will have a subtle, smoky flavour. And that's not all. As well as cooking inside the chimenea's fire bowl you can also cook outside by using the chimney as a grill or hob. You can use all these methods at the same time or mix and match to create a brilliant barbecue buffet.

COOKING INSIDE THE FIRE BOWL

Leave the chimney section in place, because the flue helps more of the fuel combust, which creates a very fine ash that radiates more heat.

- As with other forms of solid fuel barbecue, wait until the flames have died away and then spread the embers evenly over the fire grate or insulation.
- Different-sized pieces of food need different cooking times, so only cook food of the same size and thickness at the same time.
- Because the heat is supplied from both above and below food can cook very quickly inside a *chimenea*, so check items regularly.
- Juices from properly cooked meat should be clear and not pink, but use a food thermometer to make sure.
- You can also bake meat, potatoes and other vegetables by wrapping the pieces in foil and placing the parcels in the hot embers.
- Food wrapped in foil will take longer to cook than food that's directly exposed to the heat.
- You can bake beautiful 'hearth' bread, tasty tortillas and perfect pizzas inside the chimenea by using pizza stones and pizza pans.
- Use metal skewers rather than wooden ones when cooking kebabs. Metal will transfer heat into the centre of the food, whilst wooden skewers may catch fire!

COOKING ON TOP OF THE CHIMNEY

To cook on the top of the chimney you'll need a special bowl called a crown. The crown has a hole in the bottom, so that it doesn't block the flue, and a rack. You can use the crown in two ways:

- **As a grill** – place the food on the rack and cook as you would on a normal barbecue. Besides keeping the flue clear the hole allows smoke through to flavour the food.
- **As a hob** – place casseroles, sauces and other side dishes in a heatproof container directly on to the crown. You can also use a wok placed directly on to the crown to cook superb stir fries.

CLEANING AND CARING FOR CHIMENEAS

At the end of cooking let the fire burn out naturally. NEVER throw water on the fire to extinguish it, as the abrupt change in temperature can cause both clay and cast iron chimeneas to crack.

During the season, remove grime and grease from the exterior by means of a good wash with soap and water, but avoid cleaning the interior with detergent as this can taint the food. A good, hot burn-off at the start of the season, and at regular intervals, should be enough to sterilise the interior and remove any food residue from both ceramic and metal chimeneas. In addition to a burn-off you should also carry out the following maintenance tasks:

METAL CHIMENEAS

Very high heat will eventually burn away even heat resistant paint, so you should check regularly for any chips or peeling and retouch as required. As an added protection from rust, after each use wait until the chimenea is cool enough to touch safely then wipe down the outside with WD40 or a similar water-repellent oil. NEVER use oil on the inside as this will taint the food.

At the end of the season, clean any racks and other removable items and store them indoors. Remove any rust spots from the exterior and retouch any chips. If the paintwork is in really poor condition, repaint the whole exterior with a heat-resistant outdoor paint before packing the chimenea away for the winter.

www.garden4less.co.uk

www.garden4less.co.uk

Store your chimenea indoors in a garage or shed or use a proper cover. Most designs will fit under a universal cover that won't blow away in high winds – these are available from good garden centres and DIY stores and cost very little.

CLAY CHIMENEAS

At the end of the season clean any racks and other removable items and store them indoors. Frost is especially harmful for clay chimeneas, so reapply the sealant and move the chimenea into a garage or shed if you can.

If you do have to leave your chimenea outside move it to a sheltered spot and use a proper cover. Remove any sand or gravel insulation before you move the chimenea, as the extra weight could crack the clay.

⚠ Chimenea safety!

Whatever type of chimenea you own, and however you use it, all the rules relating to food hygiene and fire safety also apply.
To briefly recap:
- **Never leave a chimenea unattended once lit.**
- **Always keep a suitable fire extinguisher handy.**
- **Use a bucket of water to put out sparks that fly out of the top of the chimney and land on the lawn.**
- **Keep children and pets away from the chimenea as its outside surfaces can get very hot.**
- **Wash your hands thoroughly before, during and after cooking.**
- **Use colour-coded utensils and containers.**
- **Cook and store food at the appropriate temperature and always use a food thermometer to check the internal temperature of cooked food to make sure it's safe (see the charts on pages 66-68).**

Cooking with permanent outdoor brick ovens

A chimenea is a useful free-standing outdoor oven, but serious barbecuers who have the space may like to invest in a more permanent version of this fantastically versatile cooking device.

www.dingley-dell.com

Because permanent ovens are made of brick they're less prone to cracking and the other faults inherent in chimeneas. Also, the cooking chamber in a permanent oven can be heated to higher temperatures than in a chimenea. All these properties will help you cook food better.

All ovens have an enclosed cooking chamber that retains heat to cook food from above and below. This means that brick ovens (also called masonry ovens) shouldn't be confused with brick or masonry grills, which only cook food from below.

Oven cooking is divided into two categories, baking and roasting. The difference is that roasting involves basting (pouring any melted fat over the food) whilst baking doesn't. Basting is essential in helping to keep meat moist during the Maillard reaction which browns and caramelises food.

You can pot roast and bake food wrapped in foil on a normal gas or charcoal grill because what you're doing with these methods is using a small heatproof container to create a miniature oven. Whilst this is fine for family barbecues, if you regularly cook for large parties you may like to upgrade to a permanent brick oven. However, installing a brick oven is a major project, so before you start it's worth taking a little time to understand what's going on inside the cooking chamber, because this will help you build or buy the right oven for your needs.

HOW A BRICK OVEN WORKS

Ovens are as old as civilisation. Archaeologists have found ovens made from bricks (masonry) or mud (adobe) in ruins all over the world, and modern Italian pizza ovens (*forno*) are almost identical to the Roman 'beehive' ovens found in the buried bakeries of Pompeii.

The secret of the brick oven's success is the dome or arch-shaped cooking chamber; this is because in any oven the walls must absorb and retain as much heat as possible, then gradually release it during the baking or roasting process. An arch or dome is the perfect shape for reflecting heat around all the interior surfaces of the cooking chamber, thus creating an even temperature in all parts of the oven.

Most brick ovens, including the Spanish-American *horno*, the French *banal* and the *tandoors* of Northern India and Pakistan, are 'black ovens' that have to be pre-heated or 'fired' before any cooking can be done. To do this a wood fire is lit *inside* the cooking chamber and left to burn fiercely with the door and chimney flue open.

www.dingley-dell.com

Wood is almost always used for firing, as coal and charcoal can leave sulphurous deposits that will spoil the taste of the food. The time required for firing will depend on the size of the oven, but the minimum time needed for the walls to absorb enough heat is usually between one and two hours.

Because black ovens use this 'retained heat' method, a classic European brick oven looks like a small igloo with a short tunnel between the entrance and the domed cooking chamber. This tunnel eliminates draughts and helps the oven retain heat.

Similarly the chimney must be placed at the front of the dome, between the cooking chamber and the door, to ensure that hot gases circulate around the entire cooking chamber and don't just heat the area below the chimney before disappearing into the atmosphere.

Once the oven has been heated to the required temperature cooking can begin. Traditionally, before any food was placed inside the ashes and embers from firing were raked into a slot by the door to fall into an ash pit below, but nowadays many experts keep a small fire burning inside the oven to maintain the temperature and flavour the food with wood smoke.

If the ashes are removed, the chimney's flue and the door must be kept closed to help the oven retain its heat; however, if a small fire is left burning the chimney flue should be open a little, to ensure that the fire burns properly and there's no build-up of carbon monoxide gas.

Cooking with a brick oven couldn't be easier. All you need to do is to place your food directly on the hot hearth (floor) of the cooking chamber and leave it until it's done. Of course, since there are no knobs and dials on a traditional brick oven, and because the cooking chamber is gradually losing heat, a bit of skill is called

for in judging exactly when to put the food in and when to take it out. For centuries all cooking in brick ovens was judged by eye. Bakers tested temperatures by sprinkling some flour on to the hot hearth and seeing how quickly it went from white, to yellow, to brown. Apart from being a waste of flour, it takes a while to perfect this method by trial and error. Fortunately a good oven thermometer and a reliable clockwork timer can now take much of the guesswork out of cooking with brick ovens.

That said, a brick oven is still a living, breathing thing, so any timings and temperatures given can only ever be approximate.

There's no substitute for experimenting with your oven to find your preferred cooking regime, but here are some guidelines to get you started.

 Hazard warning!

Before going to the trouble of building a wood fired oven in your garden check that you will not be breaking the smoke control laws active in many towns in the UK.

While BBQs are exempt under these regulations, permanent structure wood fired ovens may not be, unless they are already an exempt appliance.

So firstly check that you are not in a smoke control area (see www.smokecontrolareas.co.uk)

If you are in a control area be sure to install an exempt appliance. Check out the Defra website for an up-to-date appliance list: smokecontrol.defra. gov.uk

COOKING TEMPERATURES

Immediately after a successful firing, the temperature inside the oven can be as high as 450°C (850°F). This is actually too hot for cooking so the oven should rest for around 20 minutes until the temperature falls below 400°C (750°F). As the oven cools, place different foods inside at different temperatures, for example:

At...	Description	Cook...
370°C (700°F)	Fiercely hot	Pizza.
350–320°C (650–600°F)	Very hot	Roast vegetables and baguettes.
290–260°C (550–500°F)	Hot	Roast meats and hearth breads baked without tins.
230–200°C (450–400°F)	Medium hot	Breads baked in tins and general baking.
175–150°C (350–300°F)	Warm	Sweet puddings and scones.
120–90°C (250–200°F)	Cool	Slow roasts and casseroles.
70°C (160°F)	Very cool	No cooking – warming purposes only.

COOKING TIMES – BAKING

If fired properly a brick oven will hold its highest heat for at least 90 minutes, and much longer if you keep a small fire going inside. Cooking times will vary according to the oven, the food to be cooked and the recipe, but here's a rough guide to simple bread baking times:

45–75 minutes	Soda breads and other 'quick' breads (non-yeast leavened loaves).
45–60 minutes	Basic loaves baked in pans and tins.
35–50 minutes	Hearth breads, cottage loaves and other breads baked on flat surfaces.
15–20 minutes	Rolls and buns.
15–25 minutes	Naans, pittas and other thick flat breads.
5–15 minutes	Tortillas, chapattis and other thin flat breads.

COOKING TIMES – ROASTING AND RESTING

You can follow your favourite roasting recipe with a brick oven, but don't forget to use a food thermometer to test that the internal temperature of the food is safe. Push the probe into the centre or thickest part of the food and check that the temperature's above the safe minimum indicated in the charts on pages 66-68. Also, remember to let the meat rest before carving and serving. 'Resting' is important because it allows the meat to finish cooking. Let me explain.

During roasting, and to a lesser extent during grilling, the intense heat forces the juices in the meat towards the cooler centre. Then, when the meat comes out of the oven, gradual cooling reverses this process and allows the juices to return to the outer edge of the meat. The result is tenderer, moister meat all the way through.

To rest meat, take it out of the oven and transfer it from the roasting tin to a warm plate or a board with a 'gravy groove' to let excess fat drain away. Cover the meat loosely in foil and leave it for 10 to 20 minutes, depending on size, before carving. Steaks or chops should also rest for at least two to three minutes before serving.

Top tip!

Once a roast has rested, use a very sharp knife to carve it. A blunt knife needs a lot more pressure to cut and this extra pressure will squeeze those lovely juices away from the slice you're cutting.

BUILDING A BRICK OVEN

Though brick ovens have a long association with humanity, it's fair to say that building one is not for the novice fan of DIY. This is because you'll need to lay concrete foundations and construct complicated domes and arches. Some practice with bricklaying is therefore a definite advantage.

That said, and if you do fancy having a go, you can find excellent plans for brick ovens on the Internet or in a book called *The Bread Builders* by Daniel Wing and Alan Scott. This extremely useful volume is the definitive work on the subject of building and using brick ovens and is readily available from good bookshops and websites. There's even a Kindle version.

Rather than attempting to build a brick oven from scratch you could always opt for a kit, at least for the dome. Such kits feature a set of preformed parts made from 'refractory' (heat-retaining) cement that are glued together with a special heatproof silicone. The best kits come complete with a metal door and a chimney with a cowl to keep out the rain when not in use. However, even with a kit you may still have to build the concrete base and brick supports yourself.

SEASONING YOUR OVEN

Whether you build your oven from scratch or from a kit you'll need to season it before you use it for the first time. This is to ensure that all the water is driven from the bricks and cement. Unless the cement is properly cured it could crack and crumble when you light your first large fire.

The seasoning process for a brick oven is exactly the same as for a *chimenea* but on a slightly larger scale. Over a week, build a series of five to ten increasingly larger fires, letting the structure cool completely in between. The first fire should be the size of a daily newspaper and use sticks and twigs whilst the last should use logs up to 10cm (4in) thick.

FIRING YOUR OVEN

As with all wood fires, the best way to light a fire in a brick oven is to use the pyramid method already described on page 79.

www.dingley-dell.com

As with *chimeneas*, well-seasoned hardwood is the best firewood, especially if you want to keep a small fire burning inside the cooking chamber. You can burn pine and cheaper softwoods to get the fire going, but as I've already said elsewhere, NEVER burn painted, stained, varnished or pressure-treated timber as the chemicals released by these preservatives are highly toxic.

Once the fire is burning nicely add more hardwood logs about 30cm (1ft) long and 10cm (4in) thick. The firewood should burn easily without smoke before catching fire. Continue to add wood until the flames reach the top and front of the dome. However, the fire shouldn't flare beyond the entrance tunnel or the chimney top. Once the fire is well established leave it for about half an hour, at which point a small spot at the top of the dome should start to turn white or translucent before spreading slowly downwards to the floor. This whitening means the dome is reaching optimum temperature and occurs when the accumulated carbon at the top of the dome reaches about 400°C (750°F).

Once the whitening has begun add more wood on either side of the fire to spread the heat across the hearth (floor) and towards the walls. After a few more minutes the whitening should have covered the entire dome. For a typical-sized oven this stage is usually reached about an hour after lighting the fire, and it's at this point that ashes and embers should be raked into the ash pit via the slot at the front. However, if you want to keep a small fire going forget what you've seen in pictures and push the burning embers *to each side of the oven*, not to the back.

There are two reasons for this. Firstly you'll be able to see what you're cooking more easily, as you won't be dazzled by flames in front of your eyes; and secondly the fire will burn more efficiently because cold air will have a shorter path to travel from the door. This creates better convection currents circulating around the dome and thus better cooking conditions.

Having fired your oven, all you need now is a large, long-handled spatula to put food into the oven and you're ready to cook. A proper pizza spatula is called a peel. Aluminium ones are best because they're thinner and can cut through food that's baked itself to the hearth. Sprinkle the blade of your peel with flour to help food slip off more easily.

WHITE OVENS AND GAS-FIRED OVENS

White ovens are brick ovens that have a separate firebox. The fire is kept burning in the firebox and the heat generated is transferred to the cooking chamber through wall cavities or pipes. A gas-fired brick oven, as the name suggests, is fitted with a controllable gas burner inside the cooking chamber, which provides the heat. Both such varieties are much more complicated than wood-fired versions and are best left to expert back garden barbecuers or commercial activities. Besides, where is the fun in cooking in a gas fired outdoor oven? You might as well use your kitchen stove!

Cooking with earth ovens
Get back to your barbecue roots with an earth oven

Brick ovens are the direct descendants of the prehistoric earth ovens that warmed and fed our Stone Age ancestors. The only difference is that the brick oven is a permanent structure above ground whilst an earth oven is a temporary pit below.

Like a brick oven, an earth oven uses burning wood as a heat source, but it's the earth itself that forms the heat-retaining walls. The soil beyond the immediate fired layer of the pit also acts as an insulator, helping the pit retain its heat for many hours. This ensures that food remains moist and tender.

The disadvantage with earth ovens is that they take a lot of time and effort to prepare, but if done properly this method is ideal for cooking very large food items that won't fit on your regular barbecue or into a brick oven. In the Polynesian islands of the Pacific, where the earth oven is still an essential part of the large celebratory feasts called luau (Hawaii), umu (Samoa) or hangi (New Zealand), a whole pig is the favourite item to be cooked.

In theory making your own earth oven couldn't be easier. All you need to do is dig a hole in your garden, light a fire in the bottom, place the food in the embers and cover it up again. Of course, in practice things are a little more complicated.

BUILDING AN EARTH OVEN

Even a small cooking pit needs to burn through around 45kg (100lb) of firewood to produce enough embers for cooking. This can take up to a day, and in urban areas the huge quantities of smoke produced by burning such a large amount of timber will certainly upset the local authorities as well as the neighbours. Besides the smoke, you'll need to cook the food for between 12 and 20 hours, so if you're planning on experimenting with pit cooking you'll need to set aside at least two days of your life!

That said, if you have the time and need to cook something very special for a large gathering, such as a major anniversary or village fete, then a whole pig pit-cooked in the Hawaiian *kalua* style is a grand opera in the Theatre of Barbecue.

So if you live far from clean air laws and other prohibitions on bonfires, and fancy literally going the whole hog for your friends and neighbours, here are a few guidelines:

- **Digging** – dig a pit roughly 1.5m long by 1m wide by 60cm deep (5ft by 3ft by 2ft), or big enough to hold the whole hog. Save the soil, as you'll need it later. If the pit site is on grass, it's a good idea to cut away the turf before you start digging so that it can be replaced when you refill the pit after cooking.

- **Lining** – to prevent the pit collapsing line it with breeze blocks or house bricks. If you're using old bricks remove any mortar, as cement can become toxic when burned. Lining the floor with stones is optional, but if you do so, use stones the size of your head that haven't been in the sea; sea-washed stones will shatter.

- **Lighting** – build a fire in the bottom of the pit using a mix of softwood to keep it going, and dry, well-seasoned hardwood for the heat – beech is ideal. As with all cooking fires, NEVER burn painted, stained, varnished or pressure-treated wood.

- **Firing** – let the fire burn fiercely and keep adding wood until you have enough red hot embers to fill the pit up to a level in line with the top of the first course of bricks or halfway up the first breeze block. Be warned, this takes a lot of wood and up to a day to do properly.

- **Wrapping** – whilst you're waiting for the embers to accumulate, wrap each piece of food, including any vegetables and potatoes, separately and tightly. Use banana leaves for authenticity but foil is more practical. Wrapping is necessary to keep dirt out and moisture in. For a whole pig, use chicken wire to keep the foil in place but be careful not to puncture it. Traditionally, hot rocks heated in the fire are placed inside the body cavity of a whole pig, but this makes wrapping difficult and is therefore optional.

- **Loading** – when the flames have died down, rake the embers into a level bed and put the parcels of food on top. To make loading easier use sheets of expanded metal to act as slings. These slings should be long enough to span the width of the pit and to turn the edges up to form handles. Then you can lower the food gently into the pit and retrieve it easily. However, be sure to use heatproof gloves at all times when loading and douse the slings with water immediately after use, as they'll be very hot.

- **Covering** – place sheets of corrugated iron or a series of planks soaked in water over the whole length and width of the pit to form a tight-fitting lid. The lid should overlap the edge of the pit at ground level.

- **Burying** – cover the lid with a thick layer of earth to cut off any air supply to the pit. This will stop anything inside catching fire whilst retaining the heat.

- **Cooking** – leave the pit covered for between 12 and 20 hours. The time will depend on the size of the pit NOT the largest item

Stones can be heated in the fire to help cook the food in an earth oven

being cooked. Traditionally food is put in the pit the night before the feast so that it's ready for the next day. Provided the food is wrapped tightly it should stay moist and tender for many hours after it's 'done'.

- **Warning** – keep pets, children and even other adults well away from the pit at all times – falling into a hole filled with red hot embers is a recipe for disaster!
- **Serving** – when the guests are assembled remove the earth and the lid with the utmost care to avoid any scalds from clouds of steam and smoke. Use gloves and tongs to remove the food from the pit and unwrap it. Test the food with a food thermometer to check the temperature of meat (see the charts on pages 66-68).

Top tip!

If you want to use an earth oven to cook a whole pig for a special occasion you must make at least two or three practice runs first. If you don't you risk a lot of disappointed guests, considerable personal embarrassment, and entirely ruining the birthday/ anniversary/village fete!

Cooking with Southern barbecue pits

Though the phrase 'Southern barbecue pit' is a common enough term across America's Barbecue Belt it's something of a misnomer. This is because most of these 'pits' aren't earth ovens but permanent masonry structures built above ground.

When it comes to cooking, these pits grill like a normal barbecue rather than roast or bake as in true pit-cooking, but what differentiates the Southern barbecue pit from gas or charcoal barbecues is the fuel. Though there are gas varieties available, complete with faux logs, the true Southern barbecue pit has to burn wood, especially the hickory and mesquite so loved by outdoor chefs south of the Mason–Dixon line.

Southern barbecue pits come in all sizes, from small cast iron cauldrons designed for camping to large brick structures the size of a tractor wheel, but the common denominator is that such pits are usually round. This is not just to differentiate brick pits from rectangular brick grills – the curves of a circular pit actually reflect the heat back into the core of the fire. This helps the wood burn more thoroughly, producing hotter embers that will help you cook better.

LIGHTING AND CONTROLLING A PIT FIRE

As with other forms of solid fuel barbecue, light the fire using the pyramid method. You can use scrap softwood and larger pieces of timber than in other wood-burning barbecues, but let me repeat again that you shouldn't burn anything that's been painted, varnished or otherwise treated with chemicals.

You'll also need a simple toolkit to tend the fire once lit. Heatproof gloves are essential, as are a good poker and a set of fire tongs. These should be the longest you can find because ordinary-sized tools designed for indoor fireplaces won't be long enough. I also keep a garden rake with a metal head handy so that I can rake the embers around the pit to create different cooking temperatures.

Another useful tool is a steel or iron hook with a long handle. This simple device can help you move larger logs around the pit and retrieve billycans and other cooking vessels from the embers. The hook should be at least 1m (3ft) long and have a wooden handle.

A set of bellows will be very useful, especially if you've built a small ventilation tunnel into the wall. If not, a length of steel pipe fitted over the nozzle of the bellows will help direct a jet of air to the centre of the fire – but use gloves and be careful, because the end will get hot.

COOKING IN A FIRE PIT

As you've probably noticed, the plans given don't have a grill or grating to hold food whilst it's cooking. This is because if you cement a grill in place you can't add any fuel to the fire!

To create a cooking surface you simply place over the top of the pit either a metal grating to form a grill, or a steel plate to form a griddle. If you can't find something suitable in a garden centre or DIY store, ask your local blacksmith to make you one. If you want to be really clever the grill or griddle should be made in two halves so that one side can be removed to give access to the fire.

With the grill or griddle placed over the pit you cook food just as you would with a normal gas or charcoal barbecue. Wait for the flames to die down, use the heat from the embers to grill the food and move food around the cooking area to find the optimum temperatures.

If you can't be bothered to go to the expense of a custom-built grate or griddle you can use a range of implements designed for campfire cooking, such as pie irons, grid irons, billycans and skewers plus a pair of supports. The supports can be made quite easily from two lengths of steel or iron bar. A metal rebar used for reinforcing concrete is ideal and readily available from builders' merchants in suitable lengths and diameters. The bars can be of different lengths but one should be long enough to span the centre of the pit. These bars will get hot, so each end of each bar should be fitted with a square wooden handle both to prevent burns and to stop them rolling around the top of the pit.

To make these support bars, take two blocks of wood at least 20cm (8in) long and use a spade drill bit to bore a hole into one end of each block to a depth of two-thirds of its length. The hole diameter should be very slightly less than the diameter of the rebar so that it will grip the metal. Then hammer the blocks on to each end of the rebar to form the heatproof anti-roll handles.

When cooking, place these bars across the fire pit at different points and use them to support skewers, grid irons, pie irons, grill baskets and billycans as shown in the diagram below.

SKEWERS

Place food on metal skewers (wooden ones may catch fire), which should be at least 60cm–1m (2–3ft) long. To make kebabs I cook food of the same type on the same long skewer then mix and match the pieces on smaller skewers for serving. This stops the veg burning before the meat's done and so on. To ensure the flavours still mingle as on small kebabs, alternate the long cooking skewers whilst cooking – for example, meat then veg, then meat, then veg etc.

Skewers are also ideal for cooking sausages, if they're thick enough to be skewered without bursting and if you thread them lengthways so that the metal of the skewer helps transfer heat to the centre of the sausage.

GRID IRONS AND PIE IRONS

Simply load the grid iron or pie iron and place over the glowing embers. Turn as necessary.

BILLYCANS AND GRILL BASKETS

The billycan is used for pot roasting. Simply put the food in the pot, close the lid and hang in the flames or over hot embers. The grill basket is used for grilling, especially small pieces of food. Use two or more grill baskets for different foods, for example one for meat and one for veg.

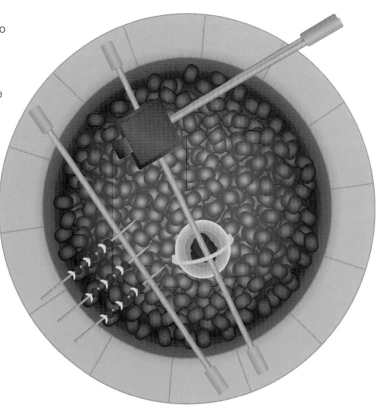

PIT SAFETY

I make no apologies for repeating my warnings that the usual food hygiene and fire safety rules also apply to pits. Always wear gloves when handling hot metal tools (a tea towel won't do), keep a suitable fire extinguisher handy (you can use water on wood fires) and use a food thermometer to make sure food is cooked properly before serving.

Top tips!

To control the temperature in a pit, use a garden rake with a long handle and metal head to rake the embers around.

Lay the fire bricks with narrow, regular joints, but lay the decorative facing stones and capstones with wide joints in a 'crazy paving' pattern. For added ventilation leave a narrow gap at the base of the wall and line this tunnel with firebricks. The tunnel should reach right through the first course of facing stones and firebricks so that there's a passage from the inside to the outside. Besides assisting in drainage you can use this tunnel to blow air into the fire with a set of bellows.

Small spits and rotisseries

Using spits and rotisseries with fire pits, brick grills and ordinary gas and charcoal barbecues.

FIT A SPIT TO YOUR PIT

Skewers are too thin to hold a leg of lamb, a whole turkey or a haunch of venison, so if you want to roast joints and other large items with any barbecue you'll need a spit-roasting rotisserie.

A spit is simply a thicker, stronger skewer designed to hold heavier pieces of food. Technically the word spit refers to just the rod to which the food is attached, whilst rotisserie refers to the whole mechanism and method of roasting on a spit. In the past spits were variously turned by waterwheels, clockwork and dogs or small boys encaged in treadmills that resembled giant hamster wheels. Thankfully electric rotisseries are far more popular nowadays.

Fitting a rotisserie couldn't be easier. All you need to do is screw two metal spit supports to the walls of the cooking area to hold each end of the long metal rod that forms the spit, then attach a motor to take the arm-numbing effort out of turning a spit by hand.

You can buy battery-operated rotisserie kits designed for most sizes and types of barbecue, both free-standing and permanent. Leisuregrow barbecues sell a family-size rotisserie and R.H. Hall sell a commercial Crown Verity rotisserie (see list of websites at the end of this book).

A good kit will come with all you need to fit the rotisserie to your grill, and all you have to do is simply follow the manufacturer's instructions. But here are a few points to watch for:

Put a tray underneath the meat and use the collected juices for basting

- Choose a model with sturdy 'skewer forks' to hold the food in the centre of the spit. These forks should have three prongs to hold the food securely and locking screws to stop everything sliding along the spit.
- Choose a model with an automatic reverse feature to save on motor wear and prevent food burning.
- When fixing the spit supports to the walls, make sure it will be level when you've finished or the meat may slowly slide to one end!
- For a circular fire pit, make sure the supports are fixed so that the spit crosses the pit at the exact centre of the circumference. This is to ensure the spit fits into the slots at 90°. If the spit is at any other angle to either support it won't turn properly.
- Tilt the support opposite the motor so that the back of the slot for the spit is a few degrees below the horizontal. This will stop the spit slipping out of its slot during cooking.
- Make sure you allow enough space between the spit and the top of the barbecue's wall to fit the motor.
- Don't overload the spit when cooking and always follow the manufacturer's instructions.

COOKING WITH A ROTISSERIE

This could hardly be easier. Apply any marinades or rubs to the joint, insert the spit into the centre of the meat, and fix it in place with the skewer forks. All that's left to do is place the spit in the rotisserie and wait.

You can cook any joint of meat on a spit, but un-boned, rolled joints of beef, lamb and pork are best for beginners, as they cook nice and evenly, are less likely to fall off the spit and will even baste themselves. The fact that meat self-bastes is one of the great advantages of using a rotisserie. As the spit turns the juices drip towards the bottom, but friction carries a certain amount of these juices back to the top before they can drip into the fire. In other words, the meat is always revolving in a sleeve of its own juices! And because they're cylindrical, rolled joints self-baste the best.

If you're cooking irregular joints, such as whole birds or legs of lamb, you might like to apply some extra baste to 'sheltered' areas that don't receive any dripping. Simply collect some of the juices in an aluminium foil tray placed under the joint and baste as you would in an indoor oven.

Self-basting should ensure the meat cooks evenly, but you can also rake the embers to the back of the grill (or to one side of the pit) so that as the spit turns the meat has a chance to cool and heat alternately. This will help prevent burning and ensure the centre cooks as well as the outside.

As ever, follow the proper food hygiene and fire safety precautions when using a spit and rotisserie.

SPIT BASKETS

A modern twist on the traditional spit is the fixed basket and the tumble basket. Both these devices fix to the spit and let you cook small items, such as chicken portions and vegetables, on your rotisserie as well as large joints. The fixed basket holds sausages, burgers and smaller pieces of food in a clamp so that they remain fixed as the spit turns. By contrast, the tumble basket allows food to tumble about inside whilst the spit turns.

The theory with each type of basket is that they allow smaller food items to benefit from the same self-basting process normally reserved for large joints. The tumble basket goes a step further; here the idea is that you put garlic, peppers and onions in with the meat so that the juices from the meat and the vegetables mingle as the foods tumble over each other. A tumble basket is especially good for cooking chicken and turkey pieces.

SPIT COOKING TIMES AND TEMPERATURES

Because the performance of barbecues and the sizes of joints vary so much it's impossible to give general cooking times and temperatures for spit roasting. Therefore the best way to check if meat is done is to use your trusty food thermometer to monitor its internal temperature. See the charts on pages 66-68 for minimum safe cooking temperatures.

A rotisserie barbecue from Leisuregrow

CHAPTER 7

GOING THE WHOLE HOG

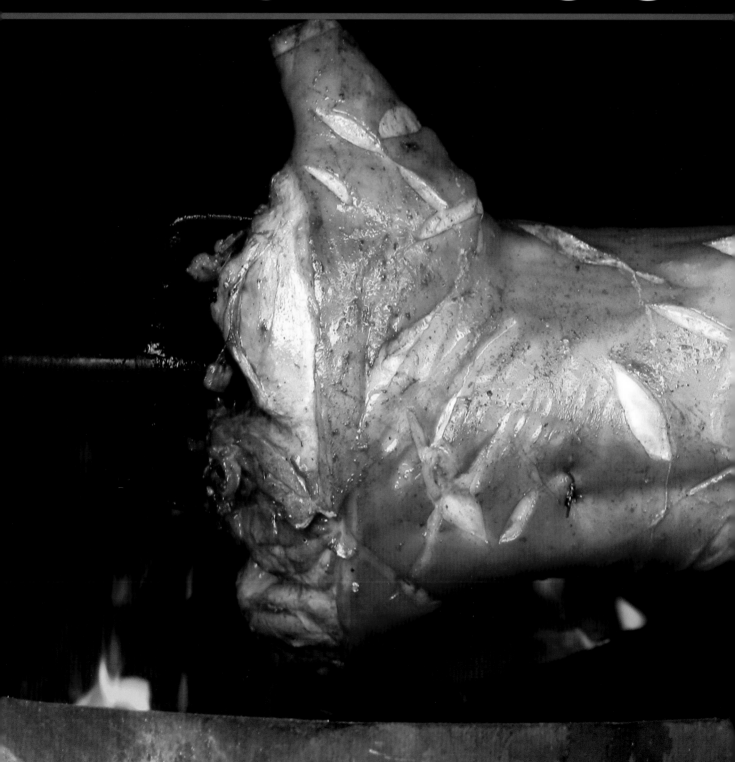

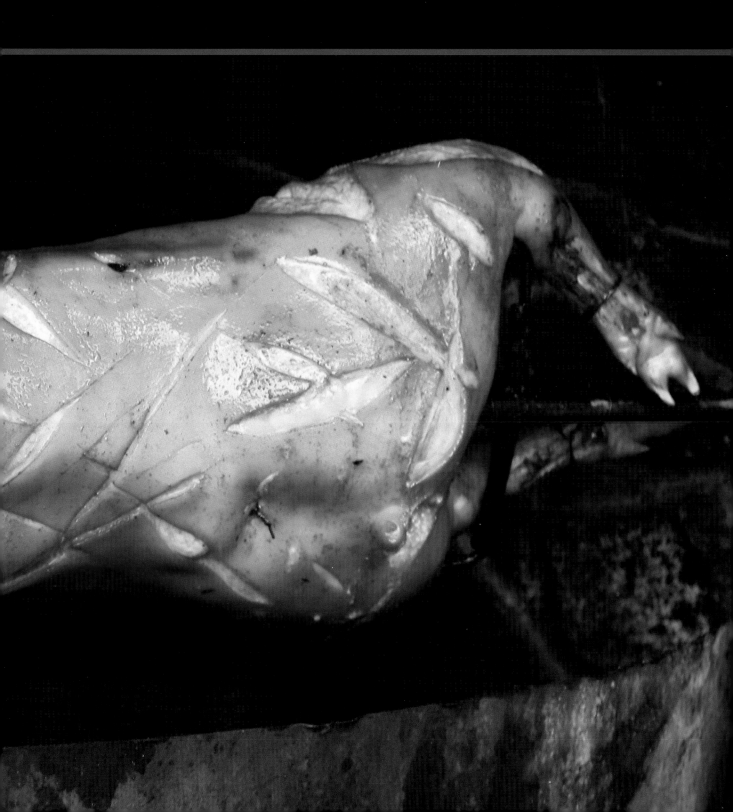

ALL THE FACTS YOU NEED

Hosting a hog roast

Without doubt the Mount Everest of back garden barbecuing is the hog roast, where a whole pig is spit-roasted over an open fire. Footballers aspire to appear at Wembley and tennis players want to win Wimbledon, but anyone serious about barbecuing will hope to do a hog roast at least once in their outdoor cooking career.

Unfortunately a fully-grown pig can weigh over 90kg (200lb) and measure 1.8m (6ft) from snout to tail. That's a lot of meat to spit roast on a back garden rotisserie, so if you do want to cook a whole pig, lamb or other large beast you're going to need some specialist techniques and equipment.

START WITH A SUCKLING PIG

A suckling (or sucking) pig is simply a piglet aged between two and six weeks that hasn't yet been weaned. Because it's been fed only on its mother's milk, a suckling pig's meat is paler, more tender and tastier than pork from an older animal.

Suckling pig is therefore highly prized and has been a centrepiece of dining tables for centuries. Spit-roasted suckling pig is still a particular delicacy in Spain and Spanish-speaking countries, where it is called *lechón*. This popularity has its roots in the Middle Ages, when during the long series of wars between the Christian and Muslim districts of Spain, called the Reconquista, the Islamic prohibition on consuming pork meant that eating, or not eating, suckling pig became an important test of religious faith.

Nowadays suckling pigs are popular on both sides of the Atlantic because they're considerably smaller than the adult

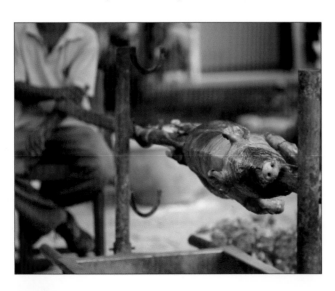

animal and can be spit-roasted on a back garden barbecue quite easily. However, check the manufacturer's instructions about the maximum weight your rotisserie can cook before buying your suckling pig.

I recommend starting with a suckling pig that weighs around 11kg (25lb), which will serve about 15 people. For smaller numbers, a practical and more reasonably priced alternative is a pork shoulder joint, which is easy to cook on a gas-fired barbecue with a lid and not only creates that great hog-roast taste but also preserves the sense of theatre that's an essential element of any whole hog roast.

If you're cooking smaller joints, take a look at the Leisuregrow range of gas-fired barbecues which are available in several sizes and come complete with Grillstream Technology. The Grillstream system, which can be fitted to gas or charcoal grills, consists of a patented rack that channels fat and oil away from food to create healthier meals, as well as leaving your equipment much easier to clean.

Practise your spit-roasting techniques with suckling pigs on your back garden rotisserie until you feel you're ready for the big one – a whole roasted hog fit for Robin Hood himself.

HOG ROAST: A POPULAR EVENT

In recent years spit-roasting larger pigs has became an increasingly popular feature of large gatherings such as village fetes, country fairs, pop festivals and even weddings. In Germany *spanferkel* is a popular attraction at the Oktoberfest Beer Festival, whilst in Russia and Eastern Europe spit-roasted pig is served at Christmas.

This renaissance in the popularity of spit-roasting means that if you're preparing a fund-raising feast for your local sports club, church or other organisation you can easily hire a commercial-sized spit roaster fit for cooking larger pigs. But you can also build your own quite easily.

THE FIREPLACE AND FIRE

Earlier we looked at how to roast a whole pig below ground in an earth oven, and many of the same principles apply to spit-roasting above ground.

In Argentina they cook whole pigs, sheep and even cows using the asado method, which is similar to spatchcocking a chicken. The meat is part boned, flattened and hung from steel hooks welded to a metal frame resembling a crucifix. The frame is stuck into the ground at the edge of the fire in such a way as to hold the carcass at an angle of 45° to the flames and the meat is turned only once.

For a start you're going to need a fireplace that's 15–30cm (6–12in) longer and wider than the pig you're going to cook. Any less and the edges of the beast won't cook; any more and you won't be able to reach the carcass safely to baste it and perform other tasks.

Having selected a suitable spot free of the usual obstructions and dangers, mark out your fireplace and dig a shallow rectangular trench 15–30cm deep. This should be enough to keep the fire from spreading. As with an earth oven you should line the inside of this pit, because a lining will help to reflect the heat upwards to the spit. There's no need to use bricks because large sheets of aluminium foil – the kind sold for turkeys – make a great heat-reflective surface.

If you can't dig a pit and you don't want your lawn, patio, village green or cricket club car park scorched and blackened by hot embers, build the fireplace on concrete flagstones or a thick layer of sand and use a wall of old bricks, stones, railway sleepers or other fireproof material to keep the fire from spreading to unprotected areas. Unless you're going to hog roast regularly there's no need to cement the retaining wall in place.

Once you've built your fireplace, prepare the fire as you would for an earth oven. Remember, you're going to need a lot of fuel, so make sure you have plenty available before you start. Though purists like to use wood, building and burning a bonfire that will provide enough embers to cook a whole pig can take anything from 12 to 24 hours. As a result more and more fans of spit-roasting are turning to natural charcoal (rather than briquettes), as it reaches the required temperature more quickly and then burns hotter and for a longer time than wood. Charcoal therefore creates a more controllable, less labour-intensive fire. If you still want the taste of wood smoke in your crackling simply add a log or two of hickory or apple during cooking.

If you do choose charcoal over wood here are the approximate weights of fuel you'll need:

Carcass weight (lb)	Charcoal weight (lb)	Carcass weight (kg)	Charcoal weight (kg)
65	120	30	55
75	140	35	65
100	160	45	75
125	180	55	85

Whatever fuel you use, remember that whole hog roasting is no different to other forms of barbecue, and the trick is to avoid a very fierce heat that would cauterise the outside of the carcass without cooking the inside. Once your fire has reached a cooking temperature of around 175°C (350°F), rake the embers into piles to concentrate the heat where it's needed.

For small suckling pigs, rake the embers into two lines, one either side of the carcass, so that the meat has a chance to cook and rest alternately as it rotates. For larger beasts, rake the embers to an even bed but leave the areas below the back legs and front legs slightly deeper than the area in between. This is because the meat at the shoulders and haunches is thicker and will need more heat to cook.

With the bed of embers glowing brightly you're ready to cook – so long as you've got a suitable spit.

Buying or building a suitable spit

BUYING A SUITABLE SPIT

Turning a whole pig over an open fire by hand, for 12 hours or more, is next to impossible for one person, so a battery-operated electric spit that turns the meat mechanically is essential to avoid charred clothing, singed eyebrows and blistered hands.

Thankfully there are motorised spits available that can accommodate a load of up to 90kg (200lb). My favourite is the Crown Verity Heavy Duty Rotisserie, designed for use with their 60 or 72in gas-fired grills. Crown Verity has a serious claim to being the 'King of the BBQs' thanks to their range of stylish stainless steel catering grills that are immensely popular with both professional and amateur barbecuers who want to cook for large events. Though based in Canada, the grills are available in the UK. Just go to www.crownverity.com and click on 'sales reps' for their British distributor's contact details.

BUILDING A SUITABLE SPIT

A rotating spit needs to have a round metal rod at least 2m (6ft) long and 1–2cm (0.4– 0.8in) thick depending on the size of pig you're going to cook.

The spit is inserted lengthways into the carcass via the mouth and tail. However, a simple bar will merely turn inside the meat so you also need something to secure the carcass so that it turns with the spit. If you're buying or hiring the equipment check that the spit comes with easily adjustable skewering forks and clamps that will hold the meat in place.

If you're making your own spit you'll need to fix two metal crossbars to the spit that should be at least 60cm (2ft) long and moveable to accommodate different sizes of carcass. To make these, drill a hole in the middle of each crossbar then drill four holes in two groups starting about 30cm (1ft) from each end of the spit. The holes in each group should be roughly 15cm (6in) apart and positioned around a point where the front and back of most pigs will normally sit. Don't make the holes too large or the spit will split!

Now you can bolt the crossbars at different points along the spit according to different sizes of pig, lamb or deer. Secure the carcass to both the crossbars and the spit using sturdy garden wire, but make sure the wire doesn't have plastic a coating.

If you're turning the spit by hand, bolt or weld a Z-shaped piece of metal to one end to form a crank and either fit a rounded wooden handle to insulate the metal and avoid blisters, or buy a very thick pair of gloves.

Once the spit is ready you'll need two spit supports. Ideally these should be able to support the carcass at various different heights so that it can be raised or lowered over the fire to control the cooking.

The simplest design of spit support is a pair of metal A-frames pushed into the earth. Each frame is made from two steel uprights with two or more V-shaped crossbars bolted between them. The Vs should be shallow enough to hold the spit securely so that it won't wobble when turned, but not too deep or the friction will be too

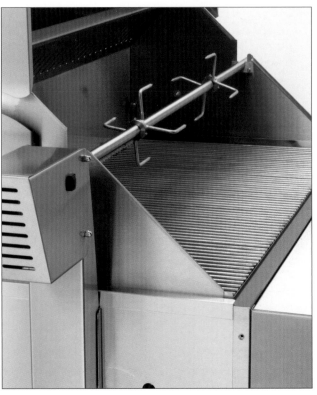

A Crown Verity professional barbecue with a spit roast attachment

great to allow the spit to rotate easily.

The A-frames' legs can be pushed into the ground, and for extra stability a metal rod slightly shorter than the spit should be bolted to the top of each frame to form a crossbeam. Use bolts rather than welds so that everything can be taken apart and stored easily afterwards. And remember to leave enough space below the crossbeam for the spit to turn freely when fully loaded.

The spit must also be able to rotate without the carcass's legs being dragged through the fire (see trussing below). Therefore the supports should be able to hold the spit at a range of heights 60cm–1.2m (2–4ft) above the fire and at least 50cm (18in) below the crossbeam fitted to the A-frames.

Top tip!

If you don't want to drill holes in your spit to attach crossbars, search the Internet or your local catering supplier's stock for a set of heavy-duty skewering forks and clamps suitable for spit-roasting whole pigs. Heavy-duty forks should have four prongs, not three, and both forks and clamps should have a screw fixing attachment that allows them to slide along the spit or be fastened firmly to it as required.

Choosing the right pig

Ask your butcher to prepare the pig for spit-roasting, which simply means that the hair and internal organs should be removed but the head and tail left on. However, with lamb and deer the head is removed.

Approximately half the carcass will be edible meat; the rest will be bone, gristle and trotter. Fortunately even hardened carnivores will begin to feel their arteries harden after eating half a pound of pork so a 13kg (30lb) pig should feed 30 people or more if you fill up everyone with spuds, salads and buns.

The optimum weight for a back garden hog roast is therefore a suckling pig weighing between 4.5–11kg (10–25lb). This is actually quite small for a whole porker, but choosing a pig between these weights means you'll be able to cook it within hours rather than days, and it should still feed 10 to 15 people with enough leftovers for two or three days of sandwiches.

For larger parties the optimum weight is 13.5–23kg (30–50lb), but this will require a hired or home-made spit as described earlier. If you want to cook for parties larger than 100 people you really ought to cook two separate pigs on two separate spits or call in the professionals.

A good butcher will probably roll out the red carpet when you announce you want a whole pig for spit-roasting and will happily advise you on the right pig for your needs. A young well-fed beast will yield the most quality meat that's moist and tender. An older pig will yield the greatest quantity and leave plenty of room for error, but there's a danger that the pork will become dry and tough if cooked for too long.

If you're worried your pig might be too small, a good way to cheat is to stuff the body cavity with extra pork joints (make sure they're boned). This will ensure that there's plenty to go round.

Top tip!

For a real treat, try spit-roasting a rare or heritage breed of pig, such as Gloucester Old Spot. Ask your local butcher about farmers in your area who raise these rare breeds.

A suckling pig is ideal for smaller parties

ALTERNATIVES TO PORK

By definition pork is the traditional meat for a hog roast but a whole marsh or hill lamb or a whole roe or sika deer can be a fantastic alternative (a whole red deer weighs a ton and would feed a small army).

The meat should have a dressed weight of between 12 and 25kg (25–55lb) and a lamb carcass should be hung for several days to tenderise the flesh. A young roe deer can be eaten as soon as the stalker returns home but an older animal will need to be hung for two or three days to acquire a gamey flavour and lose the toughness inherent in older meat.

With lamb or deer, ask the butcher to remove the head and neck. Some people like to leave the kidneys inside and present these to the guest of honour as tradition demands, but I prefer to remove them and serve them separately. With deer the liver may be eaten if it's very fresh, and is therefore traditionally served fried at breakfast after a dawn stalk.

Cook your whole lamb or deer in exactly the same way as a pig, except that it's a good idea to cover the flanks with foil. This will ensure that the leaner ribs remain edible.

Preparing the pig

A whole pig needs to be prepared by brining, for which see Chapter 5. If you just throw it on a spit to cook, the large cuts of meat will turn out bland and tasteless whilst the small cuts will become dry and tough. My favourite brine for pork is spiced herb and cider – the apples' sweetness complements the natural taste of the pork whilst the herbs and spices add a depth of flavour.

Incidentally, do you know why pork is often paired with apple? It's because in days of old pigs were kept in orchards and allowed to feed on any fallen apples that were unfit for human consumption. This gave the pork an apple taste which was enhanced by apple stuffing (see below) and brine made from apple cider.

There are dozens of recipes for cider brine, but here's a simple one:

- 8 litres (14 pints) of fresh water
- 1kg (2.2lb) of brown sugar
- 1 tablespoon of black peppercorns
- 6 whole cloves
- Cinnamon sticks
- 8 litres (14 pints) of apple cider vinegar
- 2 garlic heads (with the tops removed)
- 2 large onions coarsely chopped and with the skin left on
- 1 fennel bulb chopped into 1cm (0.4in) pieces

Multiply these quantities accordingly until there's enough brine to completely immerse the whole pig.

Place all the ingredients except the cider vinegar in a large pot and bring to the boil. Simmer for 10–15 minutes then allow the liquid to cool completely. Pour the mixture into a clean plastic bin large enough to hold 20 litres (5 gallons) and add the cider vinegar. Stir vigorously to combine all the ingredients, then add the garlic, onions and fennel. Stir again and leave for an hour or two to let all the flavours mingle.

Whilst the brine is maturing, wash the carcass inside and out then soak the whole pig – cut side down and with the front and back legs splayed – in a bath of the brine solution.

Leave the pig to soak for at least 24 hours, and longer if possible. If you don't want to use the family bath tub for this, buy a large plastic plant trough from your local garden centre, and if you only have a few hours to brine use a marinade injector to inject the thickest parts of the pig with brine.

Top tip!

If you're spit-roasting lamb add a few sprigs of rosemary to the mix. If you're spit-roasting venison replace the garlic with a handful of juniper berries or two handfuls of blackberries.

Whilst the pig is brining, decide whether you're going to cook it with the body cavity stuffed and sewn shut or left open. A closed carcass will allow you to cook and serve fabulous stuffing but it means the whole beast will take longer to cook, because any filling will insulate its inside from the heat. Open cooking will take less time, and you can always cook any stuffing separately.

Open or closed, you'll need to treat the inside of the carcass with a marinade after brining. A tasty marinade rubbed well into the flesh from the inside will help flavour the meat closest to the bone, which can sometimes become dry and bland. Here's a good recipe suitable for both pork and lamb:

- 3 tablespoons of lemon juice
- 3 tablespoons of orange juice
- 3 tablespoons of cooking oil
- 3 tablespoons of sea salt
- 2 teaspoons of black pepper
- 6 cloves of chopped garlic

After rubbing you can stuff the beast with whatever stuffing you think will appeal to your guests. Here's my favourite simple sage and apple stuffing for pork. Note that the quantities will vary according to the size of beast you plan to spit roast – those listed are for a carcass weighing 12kg (25lb):

- 1.5kg (3lb) of minced pork or sausage meat
- 500g (1lb) of cooking apples (peeled, cored and chopped)
- 2 tablespoons of cooking oil
- 2 medium onions (chopped)
- 1 clove of garlic (chopped)
- 120ml (a large glass) of dry sherry
- 2 teaspoons of lemon zest
- A good handful of fresh sage leaves (ripped)
- Sea salt and freshly ground black pepper to taste
- Breadcrumbs (optional)

Fry the onion and garlic gently in hot oil until the onion is translucent. Add the remaining ingredients and mix together lightly. If the mix is too sloppy add breadcrumbs until stiff.

Once stuffed, sew the body cavity shut with a trussing needle and proper cooking twine – ordinary string isn't strong enough and may burn. Cooking needles and twine are readily available from good cook shops and the Internet.

Now it's time to prepare the skin. If you want delicious crackling you must season the skin with salt, though pepper is optional. To do this score the skin all over the back, shoulders and haunches with a sharp Stanley knife. The scores should be one or two finger-widths apart and deep enough to pierce the

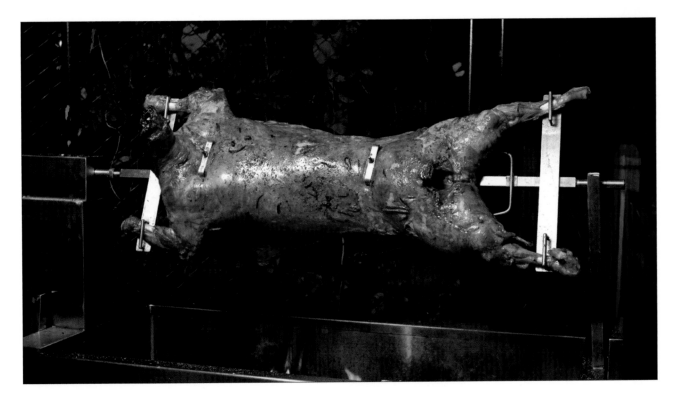

Make sure the pig is secured well on the spit

tough outer layers to reach the fat below without reaching right through to the meat.

Scoring is essential for two reasons. Firstly it helps moisture escape so that the skin dries out and creates crackling; and secondly it allows the melted fat to bubble through the skin, thus self-basting the whole pig as it turns on the spit.

Once scored, rub generous quantities of the salt and pepper mix all over the back, shoulders, haunches and flanks. Some people recommend brushing the exterior with oil as well, but provided you baste regularly this shouldn't be necessary. The secret of good crackling is to start with dry skin, score properly and not baste too much. That's all there is to it!

After seasoning the skin, the pig is ready for trussing and spitting.

TRUSSING AND SPITTING

During cooking the chemical bonds that bind flesh, sinew and bone will be loosened – which is the whole point of cooking – so good trussing is essential to keep the meat securely attached to the spit.

Spit the carcass by inserting the metal rod into the mouth (head on) or neck cavity (head off) so that it's positioned under the spine. Now push the spit through the carcass until it emerges from the tail opening between the thighs.

The spit isn't going through the muscles so the meat won't be secured to the spit. If you have a set of skewering forks and clamps, push the forks firmly into the head and rump and attach the clamps either side of the spine so that they hold the backbone to the spit.

Alternatively use uncoated metal garden wire or a large butchers' trussing needle and heavy-duty cooking twine to tie the spine to the spit every 15cm (6in) along the entire length of the backbone. Pull the wire or string as tight as possible – use pliers if you have to – and tie the knots off at the back. Cut off any excess twine so that it won't burn and taint the taste of the meat.

Some spit-roasters like to leave the legs dangling, but the spit needs to be quite high off the heat to do this successfully. I therefore prefer to tie the thighs and legs tight against the hips and the spit. The same applies for the head and shoulders; you don't want any part of the carcass to move and everything should turn as if one with the spit.

If you have a homemade spit with crossbars, remove and reattach them after spitting. Splay the front and back legs, then use wire or twine to secure the front legs to the first crossbar, wind the wire around the rest of the carcass and the spit, and secure the back legs to the second crossbar. Again, use pliers to pull the wire as tight as you can at each fastening point and twist any loose ends together.

Whatever method you use to secure the carcass to the spit, remember that the flesh will loosen, move and shrink during cooking. This means that unless the trussing is really tight the meat might fall off the spit accompanied by gasps of disappointment from your guests. To avoid this disaster, especially during your first two or three hog roasts, wrap uncoated metal chicken wire around the carcass to keep everything together until it's done.

Finally, before placing the spit over the fire cover any extremities such as ears, nose, tail and trotters with foil to prevent burning. The foil should be removed for the last hour of cooking to allow everything to brown evenly. This will create a fantastic-looking hog roast as well as perfect pork.

Cooking the pig

A pig will need regular basting

I can't say this often enough, but low and slow is the secret of all barbecuing, and spit-roasting is no exception. Pork grilled too quickly leads to burnt skin and dried-out meat, so the cooking temperature should be as close to 120°C (250°F) as possible; you can check this with a background thermometer, so it's a good idea to get one if you're going to hog-roast often.

If you have a spit with different support heights you can manage cooking times and alter the heat by raising and lowering the spit. Start with it on the highest support for an hour, then move it closer to the fire for the remainder of the cooking time. Alternatively you can control temperatures by raking the embers around the pit and adding more fuel as required.

Besides rotating the spit constantly, you also need to baste the carcass at regular intervals. Basting will help the meat become a beautiful golden brown and keep everything moist and tender, but remember that too much basting can ruin crackling.

To baste, place a large pan or a disposable aluminium-foil roasting tray below the carcass to catch the dripping fat. For large beasts, use two or three collecting vessels. Don't leave the pans or trays in the fire for too long as the fat in them may ignite. When you

have enough juices use tongs to retrieve the trays and a wallpaper brush to apply the liquid to every part of the carcass. For a really professional finish you can create your own baste by adding lemon juice, herbs and other seasoning to the melted fat. Experiment with two or three small joints to find a bespoke baste that's right for you.

Whilst cooking you also need to watch for flare-ups caused by fat dripping on to the fire and igniting. A really big flare can set light to the whole carcass, so keep suitable firefighting equipment handy. This should include a large fire blanket, a spray-gun full of clean water and a fire extinguisher suitable for charcoal and wood fires.

Besides a rake with a metal head you should also have a long-handled metal hook, a shovel or spade, long-handled tongs and a pair of heat-resistant gloves to tend the fire and the hog roast.

Now leave the carcass to cook, but be sure to allow plenty of time before the party starts. Depending on their size and the cooking temperature, whole hogs can take anything from 4 to 24 hours to cook completely so plan ahead and take your time. The chart below provides a rough guide to the time involved:

Carcass weight (lb)	Approximate cooking time (hours)	Carcass weight (kg)
65	6–7	30
75	7–8	35
100	8–9	45
125	9–10	55
200	20–24	90

BASTING

Basting will help the skin develop a gorgeous dark brown colour, create a tasty caramelised glaze and prevent the skin and surface meat from drying out. So baste your hog frequently throughout the cooking period, especially if you notice the surface getting dry.

Basting mixtures vary and can use any number of flavouring ingredients. I like to make my baste mixtures from olive oil, wine, fruit juices, herbs and lemon juice. A little honey or sugar will enhance the flavour of the baste and help the caramelisation process, but be careful not to add too much otherwise the carbon in the sugar will burn. Remember, you want caramel not charcoal!

FINISHING

When you think the roast is nearly done, test it by pushing a skewer into the thickest part of the meat. If the juices produced run clear the meat should be done, but you must use a proper caterers' food thermometer to make sure, especially if you're cooking for a function or public event.

Use your food thermometer (the ones made by Thermapen are ideal) to check the internal temperature of the meat all over, and remember that the thickest part of the carcass must be above a minimum of 75°C (170°F) before serving. For lamb the temperature must be 60°C (140°F) or above.

SERVING

Don't be impatient and carve a few slices then leave the rest to cook for a little longer. Apart from the dangers of food poisoning you risk severe burns and causing an avalanche of pork to fall into the fire! The only safe way to serve a whole hog is to wait until it's done then remove the spit from the fire and carve and serve the meat from a separate table.

Before you start to carve, remove the spit and any trussing and let the meat rest for 20–30 minutes. Now the moment has arrived. Take a long sharp knife and:

- Cut away any crackling. Use scissors to cut it into separate portions and serve separately.
- Similarly, scoop out any stuffing and place it in a caterers' chafing dish or warmed bowls to be served separately.
- Cut off the front and back legs and carve the meat from these joints first.
- To carve a leg or shoulder, cut a wedge out of the meat near the thinner end (the shank) and carve backwards towards the thicker end. Cut the slices diagonally and across the grain of the meat.
- Cut the loins from each side of the spine and slice the meat diagonally across the grain as with the legs.
- Separate the base of the rib cage from the spine and cut away individual ribs for serving separately. If you're having difficulty, a pair of heavy-duty secateurs or lopping shears will help.

CRACKING CRACKLING

The highlight of any roasted pork dish has to be the crispy rinds called crackling. Contrary to popular belief there's no magic involved in creating cracking crackling. To get the tastiest, crispest crackling you need to start with a pig that has plenty of fat under the skin. Sadly most modern pigs seem to go jogging, so most pork is lean and mean. However, if you tell your butcher you want crackling he (or she) will select a suitable porker for you.

Besides choosing the right pig the secret of crackling is to remove any moisture from the skin before, during and after cooking, so follow these simple guidelines:

- Only use dry spice and herb rubs on the skin and avoid marinades that contain sugar, as this will caramelise and burn very quickly.
- An hour before cooking finishes, apply a generous sprinkling of sea salt to the carcass. The salt will absorb any excess moisture.

Cut slices diagonally and across the grain of the meat

- For the last half hour of cooking, add dry, well-seasoned hardwood to the fire. The flames will crisp the semi-melted fat under the skin, creating perfect crackling, whilst the wood smoke will add flavour.
- If the skin still isn't crisping properly stop basting and pour a pint of cold water over the shoulders and again over the haunches. This should wash away a lot of the excess fat and cause the skin to crisp.
- If the crackling is done before the rest of the meat, remove it and serve as an appetiser or keep it warm for serving later.
- If you do cut off the crackling remember to baste the meat underneath more often to prevent it drying out.

Top tip!

If you're cooking lamb make small cuts about an inch long all over the skin and push sprigs of rosemary and garlic into alternate incisions. For venison use dried juniper berries.

CHAPTER 8

BEN'S TOP 100
BBQ RECIPES

HERE ARE 100 OF MY TRIED AND TRUSTED FAVOURITES DESIGNED TO MAKE ANY BARBECUE A GREAT SUCCESS

Meat and game

The mainstay of any barbecue is beautifully prepared meat, but nowadays your choice of farmed meat isn't limited to lamb, beef or pork. Specialist delicatessens across the UK now stock unusual meats from sustainable sources in Africa, America and Australia, so why not try ostrich, kangaroo or crocodile for your next barbecue? If you can't find these exotic delicacies don't despair, because a little help from the contents of your herb and spice rack can turn ordinary lamb, beef and pork into something truly extraordinary.

Cuts of beef

Try and buy your meat from a local butcher – it will usually be matured for longer than supermarket meat, which means it will have more flavour.

1 Rump is one of the best value full-flavoured steaks.
2 Rib-eye, also known as the Scotch fillet, is tender and full of flavour, due to the marbling of fat.
3 Sirloin has a firm texture and is rich in flavour.
4 T-Bone is a large steak with a fillet on the smaller side of the bone and a sirloin on the other.
5 Fillet is a more expensive steak, tender, mild and subtle in flavour.

Matured meat with be tender and full of flavour

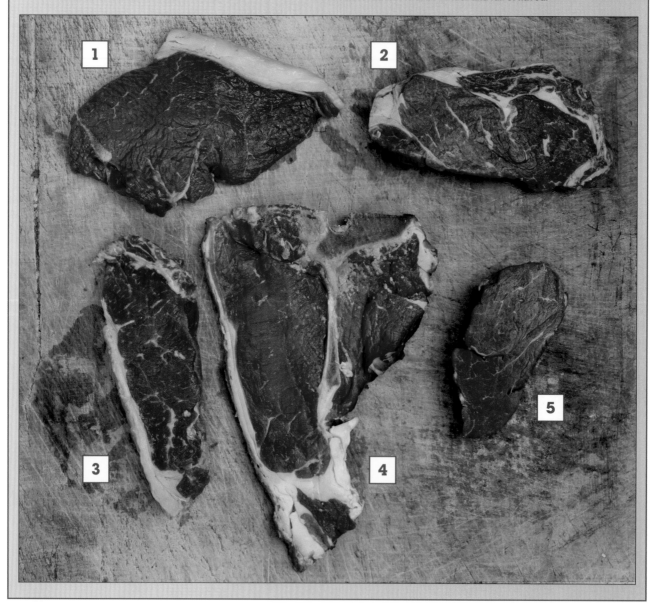

TEXAS-STYLE RUMP STEAK

Difficulty | **Serves 1**

Try this dry rub to give your steaks a terrific taste of the Old West.

1 thick rump steak (225g/8oz cut to even thickness)
1 tablespoon brown sugar
1 tablespoon sweet paprika
1 teaspoon dry mustard
1 teaspoon ground allspice
Pinch of pepper

1. Combine the first five ingredients in a small bowl.
2. Prepare the barbecue on a high heat.
3. Rub the spice mixture generously on both sides of the steak.
4. Grill the steak to your liking.
5. Serve hot.

Top tip!

This rub can be prepared up to a week in advance and stored in an airtight container until required.

ENTRECÔTE BERCY

Difficulty | **Serves 2**

The Parisian way to prepare a Great British steak.

2 sirloin steaks (225g/8oz each cut to even thickness)
Pinch of salt and pepper
6 tablespoons unsalted softened butter
2 teaspoons chopped parsley
2 teaspoons chopped chervil
2 diced shallots

1. Sprinkle both sides of the steak with salt and pepper.
2. Grill to your liking over a hot fire.
3. Over a low fire in a small pan, mix the butter with the chopped herbs and shallots.
4. Just before serving place half the butter on two hot serving plates.
5. Place the cooked steaks on top and the rest of the butter on the top of the steaks.
6. Serve very hot.

ORIENTAL BEEF KEBABS

Difficulty | **Serves 4**

Use fabulous Far Eastern flavours to spice up your steak kebabs.

500g (18oz) rump steak, cut into 2.5cm (1in) cubes
100ml (3½fl oz) teriyaki sauce
100ml (3½fl oz) dry red wine
4 tablespoons Worcestershire sauce
2 teaspoons garlic salt
½ small pineapple
1 large green pepper, cut into 2.5cm (1in) cubes
1 large onion, cut into 2.5cm (1in) cubes

1. Place the meat in one bowl and mix the teriyaki sauce, wine, Worcestershire sauce and garlic salt in a separate bowl.
2. Pour two-thirds of the sauce over the meat. Cover and refrigerate overnight or let stand at room temperature for 2 hours, stirring occasionally.
3. Prepare the pineapple by cutting into wedges.
4. Thread the cubes of meat onto four skewers, alternating with the green pepper, pineapple and onion pieces.
5. Grill over a hot barbecue for 8 minutes, then turn and grill for 7 minutes more, basting frequently with the remaining third of the sauce.

BBQ BEEF MEDALLIONS

Difficulty | **Serves 2 to 4**

This simple wet rub for beef fillets deserves a gold medal.

1 beef fillet cut into 4 medallions 2.5cm (1in) thick
150ml (5fl oz) lipsmackin' barbecue sauce (see recipe on page 169)
30ml (1fl oz) freshly squeezed lemon juice
4 garlic cloves diced
Sprig of fresh rosemary
Pinch of salt and pepper

1. Mix the barbecue sauce, lemon juice, garlic and rosemary in a bowl.
2. Season the medallions with salt and pepper.
3. Grill over a medium heat for 3 minutes on each side.
4. Meanwhile heat the sauce and brush on to each side of the medallions.
5. Grill for a further 2 minutes on each side.

AMERICAN SMOKED BEEF BRISKET AND BURNT ENDS

| Difficulty 🍴🍴🍴🍴🍴 | Serves 12 |

An all-American classic for your smoker.

5–6kg (11–13lb) whole beef brisket, fat trimmed to 1cm (0.4in)
1 tablespoon salt
2 teaspoons black pepper

1. Season the brisket with salt and pepper and allow it to rest at room temperature for an hour. Brisket cooks quicker, better and more evenly if it's allowed to rest in this way.
2. Smoke the brisket, fat side up, at 110°C (230°F) for 2 hours per kilo untrimmed weight (1 hour per pound) using apple or oak chips.
3. When the internal temperature reaches 80°C (176°F) remove it from the smoker and wrap it in foil.
4. Rest the brisket for an hour and then slice.

Top Tip

To make burnt ends, cut the fatty end of the brisket into cubes. Place these on a foil tray with the bark (blackened) side down and put back into your smoker for 2 hours at 110°C (230°F). Baste with barbecue sauce and smoke for another 30 minutes before serving.

BOURBON RIB-EYE STEAK

| Difficulty 🍴🍴🍴 | Serves 8 |

A marvellous marinade from the state of Kentucky, the home of Bourbon whiskey.

8 rib-eye steaks (225g/8oz each cut to even thickness)
2 large red onions
50g (2oz) fresh rosemary
50g (2oz) fresh mint leaves
120ml (4fl oz) Bourbon whiskey
1 tablespoon salt
200ml (7fl oz) balsamic vinegar
200ml (7fl oz) tomato juice
6 garlic cloves
100ml (3½fl oz) soy sauce

1. Combine all the ingredients for the marinade in a food processor fitted with a metal blade.
2. Place each rib-eye in a zip-lock bag and pour the marinade over it.
3. Let this sit for 2 hours at room temperature or for up to 3 days in a refrigerator.
4. Place the meat on a hot barbecue and grill to your liking.

A beef brisket with a dark smoked 'bark'

SPICY BARBECUE CHILLI

Difficulty	Serves 4

I added the barbecue sauce to this chilli recipe from my friend Gareth Williams.

1 tablespoon rapeseed oil
100g (4oz) chopped onion
100g (4oz) chopped yellow pepper
2 teaspoons chopped garlic
500g (17½oz) lean minced beef
100ml (3½fl oz) lipsmackin'
barbecue sauce (see recipe on page 169)
1 tablespoon tomato purée
1 tablespoon mustard
2 teaspoons Worcestershire sauce
1 teaspoon hot chilli powder
1 teaspoon ground cumin
Pinch of salt and pepper

1. In a large saucepan, heat the oil over a medium heat.
2. Add the onion, yellow pepper and garlic.
3. Stir for 5 minutes until softened.
4. Add the beef and cook until the mince is no longer pink.
5. Then add the barbecue sauce, tomato purée, mustard, Worcestershire sauce, chilli powder, cumin, salt and pepper. Cook gently for an hour and garnish with grated cheddar cheese.
6. Serve on nachos or rice.

30-MINUTE LAMB GRILL FOR TWO

Difficulty	Serves 2

Transform traditional lamb chops with this simple marinade.

4 lamb loin chops (225g/8oz)
1 tablespoon light soy sauce
2 teaspoons sesame oil
1 chopped onion
1 garlic clove minced
2 teaspoons chopped ginger
Pinch of salt and pepper

1. In a shallow dish, whisk together the soy sauce, oil, onion, garlic, ginger and pepper.
2. Add the lamb, turn to coat, and let the meat stand in the mixture for 10 minutes.
3. Place the lamb on a greased grill over a medium-high heat.
4. Cook for 5 to 7 minutes on each side for medium-rare, or longer if desired.
5. Salt to taste.

BASTILLE DAY LAMB WITH ROSEMARY

Difficulty	Serves 4

Next 14 July, celebrate the French Revolution with this gloriously Gallic way to grill lamb.

2.5kg (5½lb) leg of lamb butterflied (see Top Tip)
1 garlic clove minced
1 tablespoon fresh minced rosemary
1 tablespoon olive oil
2 teaspoons white wine vinegar
2 teaspoons Dijon mustard
½ teaspoon salt
Freshly ground black pepper

1. Combine the garlic, rosemary, oil, vinegar, mustard and salt in a small bowl.
2. Rub the mixture over the entire surface of the lamb and let it marinade in a zip-lock bag in a refrigerator for 4–6 hours.
3. Take the lamb out of the fridge and let it sit at room temperature for 30 to 45 minutes before barbecuing.
4. Start by grilling the leg over a medium-high direct heat. When the surface is seared, move to indirect barbecuing and reduce the temperature to medium. The leg of lamb will need about 20 minutes per 500g (approx 20 minutes per pound) to cook.
5. When the internal temperature of the meat reaches 70°C (158°F), take the meat off the fire and let it rest for 15 minutes.
6. Carve the meat, starting from the thick end and working your way down to the shank.

Top tip!

When you buy your leg of lamb, ask your butcher to 'butterfly' it for you. This boneless cut should have a centre portion and two flaps, and as this recipe uses only the centre part the remaining portions can be stored in the freezer for later use. The larger flap can be grilled whilst the smaller makes excellent kebabs. If you're cooking for a large family, use the entire leg.

HOME-MADE BEEF OR LAMB BURGERS

Difficulty	Serves 4

Forget fast food takeaways, nothing beats home-made burgers grilled on your own barbecue.

450g (1lb) lean minced beef or lamb
75g (2½oz) finely chopped onions
10ml (½fl oz) cooking oil
Sprig of chopped thyme
Sprig of chopped parsley
1 beaten egg
Pinch of salt and pepper

1. Melt the butter in a saucepan with the onion and fry over a gentle heat until the onion has softened.
2. Mix the mince, herbs and egg.
3. Mix in the onions and a pinch of salt and pepper and mould into burgers.
4. Grill the burgers on a medium heat for several minutes on each side.

SOUTHERN-STYLE PULLED PORK

Difficulty	Serves 8

Every great griller needs to have their Boston butt pulled once in a while!

3–4 kg (6–8lb) pork shoulder on the bone ('Boston butt' in the US)
50g (2oz) yellow American mustard
100g (3½oz) general meat rub (see recipe on page 164) with no sugar
100ml (3½fl oz) rapeseed oil
100ml (3½fl oz) apple juice

1. Rub the pork shoulder with the mustard.
2. Use a spice sprinkler to give the outside of the meat a generous amount of the pork rub blend.
3. Indirectly smoke the meat at 110°C (230°F) for 8 hours, turning every 2 hours so no side gets too much heat.
4. You can mop the meat with an equal mixture of the rapeseed oil, apple juice and a tablespoon of the pork rub.
5. The pork is done when the internal temperature is above 85°C (185°F).
6. Cover and rest for an hour. Then tear the pork apart and discard the bone, fat, connective tissue and gristle.
7. Pork shoulder butt can be eaten sliced or pulled.

ORIENTAL PORK AND LEMON SKEWERS

Difficulty	Serves 4

The lemongrass and soy sauce adds exotic Thai flavours to these succulent skewers.

300g (10½oz) lean minced pork
10g (½oz) finely chopped mint
10g (½oz) granulated sugar
10ml (½fl oz) light soy sauce
4 garlic cloves finely chopped
1 lemon freshly squeezed
8 lemongrass stalks
Pinch of salt and black pepper

1. Place the minced pork, garlic, mint, soy sauce, sugar and lemon juice in a large bowl and season.
2. Mix well and divide into 8 portions. Mould each one into a ball around the lemongrass stalk.
3. Barbecue the skewers on a medium heat for 6–8 minutes on each side.

Top tip!

'Pulled' refers to the method of tearing the meat apart by hand (wear disposable plastic gloves to keep your hands grease-free) or with two forks. The meat should be so tender it can be pulled easily and eaten as it is or chopped and served on a bun with lip-smackin' barbecue sauce (see recipe on page 169) as a pulled pork sandwich.

CRUIBINS (GRILLED PIGS' TROTTERS)

Difficulty ✗✗✗✗   **Serves 4**

A traditional Irish recipe that turns a humble pig's trotter into a delicacy fit for a High King of Tara.

4 brined pigs' trotters
2 carrots
1 stick celery
1 onion
150ml (5fl oz) white wine vinegar
50g (2oz) melted butter
300g (10½oz) dried breadcrumbs
Pinch of allspice

1. Get plain pigs' trotters from your butcher and brine them for 24 hours (see below).
2. Bandage the trotters with several strips of cheesecloth, or tie them several times around with string, because trotters will try with all their might to fall apart while cooking.
3. Put the trotters into a suitable pot with the vegetables, and cover with the water and vinegar.
4. Simmer gently for 6 or 7 hours then allow the trotters to cool in the liquid.
5. When cool, split each trotter in two the long way and roll in melted butter and dried breadcrumbs mixed with a pinch of allspice.
6. Heat the breadcrumbed trotter slowly on the barbecue until the outside is hot and crisp.
7. Serve with mustard and horseradish.

A BASIC BRINE FOR PIGS' TROTTERS
If you're preparing cruibins you'll need this brining recipe.

1.5 litres (2½ pints) of water
300g (10½oz) sea salt
300g (10½oz) brown sugar
50g (2oz) saltpetre (optional)
1 teaspoon juniper berries
1 bay leaf
3 sprigs thyme
1 teaspoon black peppercorns
4 cloves
Small piece of ungrated nutmeg

1. Put all the ingredients in a pan and bring to the boil.
2. Skim the top and remove from the heat.
3. Let the mixture cool and add the trotters. Weigh them down with a clean stone and leave for 24 hours.

KANSAS-STYLE BABY BACK RIBS

Difficulty ✗✗✗✗   **Serves 2**

This is a favourite way to serve 'slabs' on the prairies of the Mid-West.

2 whole racks of baby back pork ribs (called 'slabs' in the US)
General meats rub (see recipe on page 164)

1. To prepare the ribs, remove the membrane from the back and trim off any excess fat.
2. Sprinkle the rub generously all over the ribs.
3. Cover and rest in the refrigerator for 2 hours.
4. Barbecue the ribs using the indirect method at 110°C (230°F).
5. You can add natural woodchips such as apple, maple or pecan to the fire to impart a smoky flavour to the ribs as they cook.
6. Cook the ribs for 5 to 6 hours, turning them every 2 hours and spraying occasionally with apple juice.
7. The ribs are done when you can easily pull two ribs apart and the meat falls off the bone.
8. Brush liberally with your favourite hot barbecue sauce.

BUTTERFLY PORK CHOPS

Difficulty	Serves 6

The accompanying sauce can be prepared in advance and kept in the fridge for several weeks.

6 good-sized pork chops, butterflied
2 tablespoons olive oil
1 small diced onion
3 garlic cloves minced
1 teaspoon ground cumin
¼ teaspoon ground red pepper
100g (3½oz) ketchup
100ml (3½fl oz) malt vinegar
50ml (2fl oz) light soy sauce
100g (3½oz) light brown sugar
2 tablespoons Worcestershire sauce
¼ teaspoon liquid smoke

1. Heat the oil in a saucepan over a medium heat.
2. Add the onion, garlic, cumin and red pepper and stir for 5 minutes until the onion is tender.
3. Add all the remaining ingredients except the pork chops.
4. Simmer gently for 10 minutes constantly stirring until the sauce is slightly thickened.
5. Prepare a medium-hot barbecue.
6. Grill the chops until cooked.
7. Allow at least 6 to 7 minutes per side and 5 minutes before each side is cooked brush with the sauce.

CROCODILE BURGERS

Difficulty	Serves 4

Like the old joke says, 'Bring me a crocodile burger – and make it snappy!' (Crocodile and alligator are available from specialist delicatessens.)

500g (18oz) minced crocodile or alligator tail
1 finely chopped onion
1 egg
Pinch of salt and pepper

1. Mix all the ingredients together in a bowl and season.
2. Shape into 4 burgers and grill over a medium heat for 6 to 7 minutes.
3. Serve on a bun with your favourite garnishes.

Top tip!

To butterfly the pork, cut slices almost entirely through the chop to make them half as thick. Open up the two sides as if opening a book. With a flat side of a large knife, pound the pork lightly to flatten it a little.

VENISON FILLETS

Difficulty	Serves 2

A recipe for venison that's just the thing for modern Robin Hoods, Maid Marians and their Merry Men and Women.

2 venison fillets (225g/8oz each)
1 teaspoon white pepper
1 teaspoon garlic powder
1 teaspoon celery salt
1 teaspoon barbecue sauce
1 teaspoon honey
1 teaspoon dried lemon thyme

1. Wash and trim the fillets.
2. Rub with the pepper, garlic and salt.
3. Combine the barbecue sauce, honey and lemon thyme and marinate the fillets in a zip-lock bag for at least 30 minutes.
4. Roll the fillets up in foil and cook slowly on a low heat for 30 minutes.

KANGAROO KEBABS

Difficulty	Serves 2

Put the bounce back in your barbecue with kangaroo kebabs and this delicious dry rub from Down Under. (Kangaroo is available from specialist delicatessens.)

150g (5oz) of kangaroo fillet, trimmed and cubed
2 teaspoons coriander seeds, roasted and ground
1 teaspoon black pepper, freshly ground

1. Roll the cubes of kangaroo meat in the ground coriander seeds and black pepper, coating lightly.
2. Skewer the meat and put it on an oiled tray ready to cook.
3. Brush with oil and grill the kebabs over a high heat for 8 to 10 minutes, turning every couple of minutes. Be careful not to overcook the meat, as kangaroo toughens easily.
4. Remove the skewers and serve with a glass of the amber nectar!

AFRIKANER OSTRICH STEAK WITH HONEY AND BALSAMIC VINEGAR

Difficulty	Serves 4

Whether or not you are on a South African safari, this fantastic marinade will make ostrich steaks fly off the braai. (Ostrich is available from specialist delicatessens.)

4 ostrich steaks (170g/6oz each)
100ml (3.5fl oz) balsamic vinegar
4 tablespoons honey
4 tablespoons extra virgin olive oil
2 tablespoons freshly chopped basil
1 teaspoon wholegrain mustard

1. Place the ostrich steaks into a zip-lock bag.
2. Mix all the other ingredients in a jug and pour over the steaks.
3. Marinate for 4 hours.
4. Barbecue on a hot grill for 5 minutes on each side.

A quick word about sausages

All sausages are seasoned minced meat mixed with fat and stuffed into a natural or artificial casing. Since sausages are a useful way of using up small bits of meat and offal, they've been around for as long as cooking has existed, and every culture has developed its own unique recipes. But from Spanish chorizo to German bratwurst, most sausages fall into one of these three types:

- **Fresh sausages** – are filled with raw minced beef, pork, chicken or any other type of lean meat and stored uncooked in a cool place until needed. These sausages must be cooked before consumption, but once cooked they may be stored for one or two days in a refrigerator. American hot dogs and traditional British bangers are the best-known examples of a fresh sausage.
- **Cooked and smoked sausages** – as the name suggests, these are cooked then smoked to add flavour and enhance their longevity. Cooked and smoked sausages can be reheated (once) or eaten cold, but once the casing or packaging is pierced they need to be kept refrigerated. Italian mortadella is a good example of a cooked and smoked sausage.
- **Dry cured sausages** – haven't been cooked, instead they're cured (rubbed with dry salt) and dried in the air or smoke. During curing, natural bacteria ferment the meat and this retards decomposition. Dry cured sausages can therefore keep for a long time without refrigeration, provided the skin or casing is kept intact. All types of true salami are dry cured sausages.

As barbecuers we're really only interested in fresh sausages that need to be cooked, and as every banger-lover knows these come in a near infinite variety. But whether you prefer a hearty Cumberland ring, the herb flavours of Lincolnshire or a simple breakfast sausage, all sausages should be grilled on a low to medium heat, turning often. Cooking slowly and gently will help the sausages hold their flavour and prevent the outside burning before the inside is cooked.

One final tip: forget what granny used to say – don't puncture the skin, as this lets the juices leak out and renders the sausage dry and tasteless!

Poultry

Tired of tame turkey legs, dull duck and boring chicken breasts?
Try these recipes for transforming ordinary poultry into meals
to remember.

MEDITERRANEAN CHICKEN BREASTS

Difficulty	Serves 4

The wonderful aromas of thyme and honey will bring a little piece of Provence to your back garden.

4 chicken breast halves
2 teaspoons Dijon mustard
4 tablespoons white wine vinegar
2 teaspoons chopped garlic
2 teaspoons honey
1 teaspoon sea salt
1 teaspoon red pepper flakes
1 tablespoon olive oil
4 sprigs of fresh thyme

1. Place the chicken breasts in a zip-lock bag.
2. Place the mustard, vinegar, garlic, honey, thyme, salt and pepper flakes into a small bowl and stir with a fork.
3. Add the oil, a little at a time, to the marinade and whisk until all the ingredients are combined.
4. Pour the marinade over the breasts in the zip-lock bag and leave in a refrigerator for at least 2 hours, turning once or twice.
5. Lightly grease the grill rack with cooking spray and place the breasts on a preheated grill.
6. Cook until tender. Allow at least 5 to 6 minutes for each side.

Top tip!

Before cooking, wrap the chicken breasts loosely in cling film, and with the broad side of a chef's knife slightly flatten the upper portion of each breast. This will help them grill evenly.

SICILIAN-STYLE CHICKEN

Difficulty	Serves 4

The cooking traditions of Greece, Italy and North Africa meet in this beautiful baste for chicken.

4 chicken breast halves
100g (3½oz) melted butter
50g (2oz) fresh chopped basil
1 tablespoon grated Parmesan cheese
¼ teaspoon garlic powder
¾ teaspoon coarsely ground pepper
Pinch of salt
Fresh basil sprigs to garnish

1. Pepper the meaty sides of the chicken breast halves.
2. Combine the softened butter, basil, Parmesan cheese, garlic powder and salt.
3. Grill the chicken over medium coals for 8 to 10 minutes on each side, basting frequently with the cheese and basil mixture.

JAMAICAN JERK CHICKEN THIGHS

Difficulty	Serves 8

Hot 'n' spicy jerk seasoning is a Caribbean classic and an essential ingredient of any barbecue.

8 large skinned chicken thighs
2 chopped onions
70ml (2½fl oz) red wine vinegar
2 tablespoons vegetable oil
2 tablespoons light soy sauce
2 tablespoons whole allspice berries
2 jalapeno peppers cut in half
2 teaspoons salt
1 teaspoon pepper
1 teaspoon ground cinnamon
¼ teaspoon ground nutmeg

1. To make the jerk seasoning, put everything except the meat into a food processor and blend until you get a smooth purée.
2. Place the chicken thighs into a zip-lock bag with half the jerk seasoning.
3. Coat each side of the meat and refrigerate for at least 3 hours.
4. Cook the chicken on a medium heat for 10 minutes on each side or until done, basting frequently with the jerk seasoning held in reserve.

BALI CHICKEN

Difficulty	Serves 4

The Balinese name for this traditional village dish is ayam panggang mesanten.

1kg (2.2lb) whole chicken
1 teaspoon salt
250ml (9fl oz) oil
1 tablespoon lime juice
500ml (17½fl oz) coconut milk
1 teaspoon dried shrimp
4 chopped shallots
3 garlic cloves crushed
3 fresh red chillies (for paste)
1 fresh red chilli (for garnish)
2 bay leaves
1 lemongrass stalk

1. Seed and shred the chillies.
2. Crush the lemongrass with the side of a cleaver or large knife.
3. Cut the chicken in half and rub with salt and oil.
4. Grill over hot coals until done, about 10 to 15 minutes each side.
5. Slice the chicken into bite-sized pieces.
6. Wrap the dried shrimp in foil and grill each side over a moderate heat for about 2 minutes.
7. Pound the shallots, garlic, chillies and toasted shrimp into a paste. Heat the oil in a frying pan, add the paste and fry on a moderate heat, stirring for 4 to 5 minutes until dry. Be careful not to let the paste burn.
8. Whilst stirring constantly, add the coconut milk, bay leaves and lemongrass. Bring to a boil and simmer for 5 minutes to allow the flavours to blend. Stir in the lime juice.
9. Add the cooked chicken and reheat in the sauce.
10. Garnish with the shredded chilli.
11. Serve with rice and Sambal Ulek hot chilli sauce.

SPATCHCOCK CHICKEN WITH GARLIC AND LEMON

Difficulty	Serves 4

The tastiest way to cook a whole chicken on a gas or charcoal barbecue is to spatchcock (see page 123) the bird and marinate it in this tasty sauce.

1 whole chicken
2 wooden kebab skewers
25ml (1fl oz) olive oil
2 garlic cloves diced
2 tablespoons lemon juice
1 teaspoon black pepper
1 teaspoon ground cumin
½ teaspoon salt

1. Combine the oil, garlic, lemon juice, black pepper, cumin and salt in a plastic jug.
2. Spatchcock the chicken (see page 123) and place it in a zip-lock bag.
3. Pour the liquid over both sides of the meat and refrigerate for at least 2 hours.
4. Barbecue on a moderate heat for 20 to 30 minutes per side, until the internal temperature of the meat reaches 75°C (167°F) when probed with a meat thermometer. The juices should also run clear when the thickest part of the thigh is pierced.

How to spatchcock a chicken

1. Place the chicken on a chopping board so that it's resting on the breast and the larger hole is facing you.

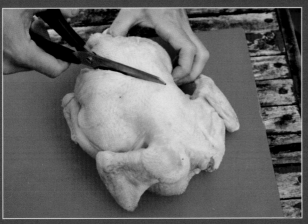

2. Use sturdy scissors to remove the backbone by cutting along each side of the spine, first the right-hand side, then the left.

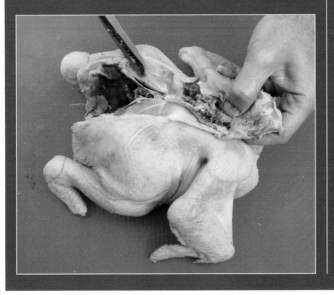

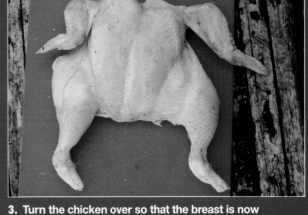

3. Turn the chicken over so that the breast is now upwards.

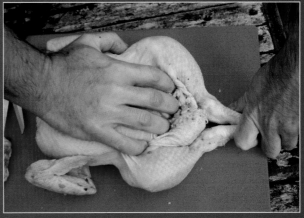

4. Use the heel of your palm to press down firmly on the chicken breast to flatten it. You will hear the ribs breaking.

5. Now secure the chicken in this position by taking some wooden skewers and pushing them diagonally through the breast, into the drumstick and out the other side.

BEER CAN CHICKEN

Difficulty 🍴🍴🍴	Serves 4

The time-honoured way to roast a whole chicken on a back garden barbecue.

1.5–2kg (3½–4lb) whole chicken
1 tall can of lager or beer
4 tablespoons general meat rub (see recipe on page 164)
50g (2oz) melted salted butter

1. Open the can of beer and pour out half the contents. Make two additional holes in the top of the beer can.
2. Remove the giblets and discard any fat inside the body and neck cavities.
3. Wash the chicken inside and out and pat dry with paper towels.
4. Sprinkle a tablespoon of the rub inside the body cavity and a tablespoon of the rub in the neck cavity.
5. Brush the outside of the chicken with half the melted butter.
6. Sprinkle the outside of the chicken with a tablespoon of the rub.
7. Stir another tablespoon of the rub into the remaining melted butter and set aside.
8. Holding the chicken upright, with the opening of the body cavity at the bottom, lower the chicken on to the beer can so it fits snugly inside. Tuck the wing tips behind the back.
9. Push the chicken down as far as it will go onto the can so it is stable.
10. Stand the chicken over a low heat, cover the grill and cook for 1½ hours until the chicken skin is crisp and dark brown.
11. Baste the chicken with the reserved butter-rub mixture every 30 minutes.
12. If the skin starts to brown too early cover the chicken loosely with foil.
13. Once cooked, place the chicken on a plate and let it rest. After 10 minutes lift the chicken carefully off the beer can and carve.

HONEY MUSTARD CHICKEN WINGS

Difficulty	Serves 2

Transform tired chicken wings into a tasty treat with this sweet'n'spicy marinade.

4 chicken wings
3 garlic cloves crushed
3 tablespoons English mustard
2 tablespoons clear honey
2 teaspoons lemon juice
4 tablespoons olive oil
Pinch of salt and freshly ground pepper

1. Place the garlic, mustard, honey, lemon juice, salt and pepper in a bowl.
2. Mix well and gradually add the olive oil. Then beat well (the lemon juice will ensure the mixture emulsifies).
3. Place the chicken and the marinade in a zip-lock bag for at least 2 hours.
4. Place on a fairly hot grill for several minutes until done and well browned.

Top Tip

Remember, never apply a marinade used for raw meat on to cooked or cooking meat. Instead divide the sauce and keep it in separate containers.

MUSTARD CRUST TURKEY BREAST

Difficulty	Serves 4

Turkey can be dry and dull, but not with this mayo-mustard glaze.

4 turkey breast cutlets (100g/4oz each)
2 tablespoons wholegrain mustard
1 tablespoon mayonnaise
1 teaspoon fresh lemon juice
Pinch of ground black pepper
1 teaspoon paprika

1. Mix together the mustard, mayonnaise, paprika, black pepper and lemon juice in a small bowl.
2. Coat both sides of the turkey with the mustard mixture.
3. Grill on a medium heat for 10–15 minutes or until browned, turning every few minutes.
4. Turkey will take a little longer to cook than chicken but should be done when the centre is no longer pink and the juices run clear.
5. Check the turkey periodically during cooking to make sure the mustard doesn't burn.

CHICKEN TANDOORI

Difficulty	Serves 6

This perennial favourite, originating from Pakistan and Northern India, is also perfect for back garden barbecues.

475ml (16fl oz) plain yogurt
50ml (2fl oz) lime juice
2 garlic cloves finely chopped
2 teaspoons salt
¼ teaspoon turmeric
½ teaspoon coriander
1 teaspoon ground cumin
½ teaspoon ground ginger
¼ teaspoon cayenne pepper
3 whole split chicken breasts
1 large onion finely chopped
1 large green pepper finely chopped

1. In a large bowl combine the yogurt, coriander, lime juice, cumin, garlic, ginger, salt, cayenne pepper and turmeric.
2. Add the chicken pieces and toss to coat. Cover the mixture with the peppers and onions.
3. Cover the bowl and chill in the refrigerator overnight.
4. Over a medium heat, grill the chicken for 15 to 20 minutes, turning every 5 minutes.

MINI CHICKEN ROLL-UP TORTILLAS

Difficulty | **Serves 4**

Take your taste buds south of the border with this classic Tex-Mex marinade for chicken breasts.

4 boneless and skinless chicken breasts
2 tablespoons olive oil
2 tablespoons lime juice
1 garlic clove diced
225g (8oz) grated mature Cheddar cheese
8 softened flour tortillas
50g (2oz) chopped onions
100ml (3½fl oz) sour cream
Pinch of salt and pepper

1. Cut the chicken breasts in half lengthways and season.
2. Combine the oil, lime juice and garlic in a bowl.
3. Marinate together in a zip-lock bag for at least 30 minutes.
4. Barbecue the chicken for 10–12 minutes, turning once, until the chicken is just cooked.
5. To make each roll-up, sprinkle a tablespoon of cheese on the lower third of the tortilla.
6. Lay one chicken strip across and sprinkle with a little chopped onion.
7. Fold in the sides of the tortillas, roll up tightly and wrap in foil (these can also be made in advance and refrigerated).
8. To serve, warm the roll-up parcels on the barbecue for 8 to 10 minutes, remove from the foil and cut in half diagonally.
9. Serve with a choice of dips.

BARBARY DUCK BREAST WITH PLUM SAUCE

Difficulty | **Serves 4**

Barbary Ducks are leaner than other domesticated duck varieties, making them perfect with plum sauce and this simple marinade.

4 180g (6oz) Barbary Duck breasts

MARINADE
150ml (5fl oz) dark soy sauce
4 teaspoons olive oil
Sprig of rosemary
Sprig of thyme
2 garlic cloves finely chopped

PLUM SAUCE
200g (7oz) plums
100ml (4fl oz) honey

1. For the marinade, mix 50ml (2fl oz) of dark soy sauce with the olive oil.
2. Add the rosemary, thyme and garlic and pour over the duck breasts in a zip-lock bag.
3. Marinate for at least 30 minutes.
4. Grill for 5–6 minutes, sealing the outside skin.
5. Place the duck breasts in a baking dish.
6. For the plum sauce, mix together the plums, remaining soy sauce and honey and pour over the chicken breasts.
7. Cook for 30–40 minutes on an indirect heat until the duck is cooked (the plum stones will drop to the bottom of the dish).
8. Slice the duck breasts and pour over the remaining sauce.

Fish and shellfish

Many back garden barbecuers believe fish and shellfish are too delicate to cook over an open flame, but these recipes will ensure your fish don't become dry and bland.

AUSTRALIAN GRILLED FISH

Difficulty	Serves 4

Contrast this spicy recipe's ginger and hot cayenne pepper with a cool Aussie lager or oaked chardonnay white wine.

4 swordfish, halibut or salmon steaks (200g/8oz, cut 1.5cm/½in thick)
50ml (2fl oz) lime juice
2 tablespoons vegetable oil
1 teaspoon Dijon mustard
2 teaspoons grated fresh ginger
¼ teaspoon cayenne pepper
Pinch of black pepper

1. In a bowl, combine the lime juice, 1 tablespoon of oil, ginger, cayenne pepper and a pinch of freshly ground black pepper to taste.
2. In a zip-lock bag, marinate the fish in the marinade for 45–60 minutes, turning 2–3 times.
3. Brush the grill with a tablespoon of oil.
4. Grill each side of each fish steak for 4–5 minutes or until cooked through – the flesh should be opaque in the centre.

GLAZED TUNA STEAKS

Difficulty	Serves 4

A brilliant way to barbecue the 'steak of the sea'.

500g (1lb) tuna steak cut into quarters
100ml (3½fl oz) dry sherry
1 tablespoon minced ginger
1 tablespoon light soy sauce
1 teaspoon honey
1 garlic clove minced

1. Combine the sherry, ginger, soy sauce, honey and garlic in a plastic jug and place the tuna steaks in a zip-lock bag.
2. Microwave the uncovered mixture on high for 1 minute or until it boils.
3. Let it cool slightly, pour half the marinade over the tuna then chill for 2 hours.
4. Preheat the grill and arrange the tuna so that the thickest part of each steak is on the outside.
5. Grill for 4 minutes and turn the steaks over.
6. Baste with the remaining marinade and grill for another 4 minutes.
7. Serve immediately.

MARGARITA SEA BASS

Difficulty	Serves 4

Inspired by the famous Mexican cocktail, this tequila-based marinade is a perfect partner for this celebrated fish.

8 sea bass fillets (100g/4oz each)
100ml (3½fl oz) white or gold tequila
120ml (4fl oz) Cointreau
150ml (5fl oz) fresh lime juice
1 tablespoon salt
3 garlic cloves crushed
3 teaspoons vegetable oil
Pinch of freshly ground black pepper

1. Place the fish in a zip-lock bag.
2. Combine the tequila, Cointreau, lime juice, salt, garlic and 2 teaspoons of oil and pour over the fish.
3. Marinate for 30 minutes at room temperature, turning occasionally.
4. Heat the grill to very hot.
5. Remove the sea bass and pat dry.
6. Brush lightly with 1 teaspoon of oil and grind some pepper over the surface of the fish.
7. Grill for 3–4 minutes per side.

How to prepare a whole fish

1 Scrape away scales with the blunt edge of a knife, moving from tail to head.

2 Rinse the fish under running water.

3 Take hold of the gill flaps.

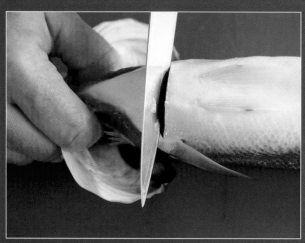

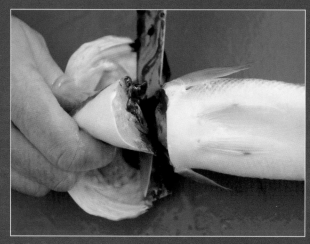

4 With a sharp knife cut just above the fins.

5 Cut through to the base.

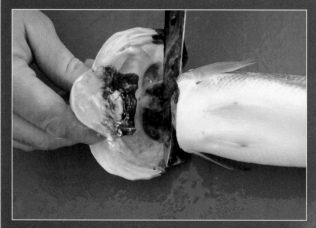

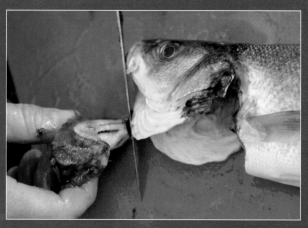

6 Cut towards the head.

7 Pull the internal parts from the skull.

8 The head contents have been completely removed.

9 Insert the tip of the knife into the middle of the base of the fish.

10 Cut up towards the head.

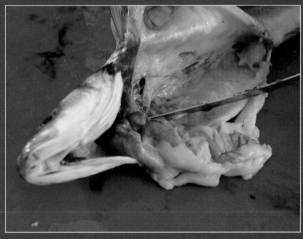

11 Remove the guts and gore from inside.

12 Wash under a running tap.

13 Remove the gills.

14 One prepared whole fish.

How to fillet a fish

1 Using a sharp filleting knife, insert mid-way through the top side of the fish.

2 Slice through the fish.

3 Pull through to the tail.

4 Pull the top fillet away from the tail.

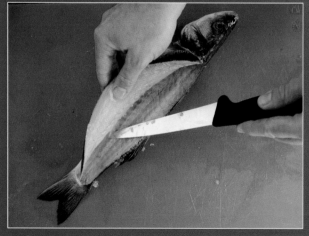

5 Use the tip of the knife to cut above the spine.

6 Gripping the tail, pull the knife through to the head.

7 Remove the fillet completely.

8 Turn over and cut off the head just behind the gills.

9 Insert the knife into the side of the fish.

10 Turn over and remove the rib bones.

11 Remove any remaining bones.

12 Fillets are ready to be used.

LANGOUSTINES

Difficulty ✗✗✗ **Serves 4**

Whether you call them Norway lobsters or Dublin Bay prawns, you'll love langoustines barbecued like this.

16 langoustines in their shells, but heads removed and de-veined
1 juiced lemon
1 large red chilli, seeded and finely diced
2 garlic cloves finely diced
150ml (5fl oz) extra virgin olive oil
Pinch of rock salt and freshly ground black pepper

1. If frozen, defrost the langoustines thoroughly.
2. Butterfly the langoustines by cutting them through the back, then turn them over and press flat.
3. Place the langoustines in a zip-lock bag with all the ingredients and marinate in a fridge for 2 hours.
4. Cook on a hot barbecue for 2 minutes, shell-side down.

TUNISIAN-STYLE KING PRAWNS AND TOMATO RELISH

Difficulty ✗✗✗ **Serves 4**

Serve your piping hot prawns with this cool and refreshing relish from the desert sands of the Sahara.

16 whole king prawns, split open and de-veined
2 teaspoons harissa paste
4 tablespoons extra virgin olive oil
1 tablespoon lemon juice

TOMATO RELISH

2 large ripe tomatoes diced
140g (5oz) diced shallots
1 large Spanish onion diced
2 teaspoons chopped coriander
1 teaspoon ground cumin

1 tablespoon chopped garlic
2 tablespoons chopped capers
2 tablespoons lemon juice
2 tablespoons light olive oil
Pinch of sugar

1. Combine the harissa paste, olive oil and lemon juice and baste the cut flesh of the prawns.
2. To make the relish, combine all the ingredients in a bowl, toss lightly and leave for 20 minutes.
3. Grill the prawns for a couple of minutes, turning once, and serve with the tomato relish.

GRILLED HALIBUT

Difficulty ✗✗ **Serves 4**

A sweet and sour glaze that's delicious with this delicately flavoured flat fish.

4 halibut steaks (225g/8oz, cut 3cm/1in thick)
100ml (3½fl oz) light soy sauce
1 teaspoon grated ginger
50g brown sugar
1 garlic clove chopped
1 teaspoon dry mustard

1. Mix all the ingredients in a plastic jug.
2. Place the halibut in a zip-lock bag with half the mixture and marinate for 4 hours, turning frequently.
3. Oil the grill and cook the steaks on a medium heat for 10 minutes, turning once. Baste with the remaining marinade frequently.

MARINATED SEAFOOD KEBABS

Difficulty 🍴🍴🍴	Serves 10

A symphony of seafood on a skewer.

450g (1lb) fresh boned and skinned salmon fillet
450g (1lb) fresh tuna
450g (1lb) fresh swordfish
450g (1lb) large prawns (peeled and de-veined)
500ml (17½fl oz) olive oil
125ml (4fl oz) fresh lemon juice
25g (1oz) fresh horseradish
25g (1oz) Dijon mustard
2 tablespoons freshly chopped dill
Salt and freshly ground black pepper
You will also need about 20 long bamboo skewers

1. Make two marinades by placing half of the olive oil and half the lemon juice together in one bowl and half in another. Add the dill to the first bowl and the horseradish and mustard to the second but season both with salt and pepper.
2. Cut the salmon, tuna and swordfish into 1.5 x 1.5 x 5cm (½ x ½ x 2in) pieces.
3. Place the salmon and the swordfish in the horseradish-mustard marinade and the shrimp and tuna in the dill marinade for about 30 minutes.
4. While the seafood marinates, soak the bamboo skewers in cold water to help reduce burning.
5. Thread the seafood on the skewers, alternating each type of fish but beginning and ending with a prawn.
6. Grill over a hot grill for about 4 minutes, turning occasionally.

BARBECUED OCTOPUS

Difficulty 🍴🍴	Serves 4

A superb sauce to transform ordinary octopus into something special, and best of all there's a bit of leg for everyone!

400g (14oz) octopus cleaned and cut into pieces
500ml (17½fl oz) tomato sauce
2 chopped chillies
3 garlic cloves chopped
100ml (3½fl oz) olive oil
100g (3½oz) sugar
Dash of Worcestershire sauce

1. Place the octopus pieces in a bowl and mix with half the oil.
2. Mix the remaining ingredients in a separate bowl.
3. Grill for two minutes, brush with sauce then cook till tender.

How to de-vein prawns

1 Using a sharp knife, cut the head from the body.

2 Gently pull the tail from the body without removing the flesh.

3 Peel off the shell around the body.

4   Check all the shell has been removed.

7   Gently start to pull out the vein.

5   Take the tail in one hand and straighten out the body.

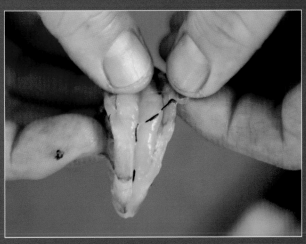

8   Continue along the prawn until all the vein has been removed.

6   Cut along the side of the vein.

9   One de-veined prawn ready for the barbecue.

RAJ'S SPICED FISH

Difficulty	Serves 4

This recipe is inspired by my BBQ buddy Raj Jethwa, who makes the most fantastic garam masala by slow roasting, grinding and combining peppercorns, cloves, Malabar leaves, mace, black cumin, cardamom, cinnamon, nutmeg, star anise and coriander.

4 skinned sole fillets (120g/4oz each)
600ml (20fl oz) plain yogurt
8 teaspoons garam masala
4 teaspoons ground coriander
8 garlic cloves crushed
2 teaspoons chilli powder
4 tablespoons lemon juice
1 tablespoon salt and pepper
Lemon wedges for garnish

1. Rinse the sole, pat dry with paper towels and place the fillets in a zip-lock bag.
2. Sprinkle with salt and pepper.
3. Mix together the yogurt, coriander, chilli powder, garlic and lemon juice.
4. Pour over the sole and refrigerate for 2–3 hours.
5. Transfer the fish to a fish rack and barbecue for 8 minutes or until the fish just begins to flake. Turn halfway through cooking.
6. Garnish with lemon wedges.

GRILLED SHARK

Difficulty	Serves 8

This is a real treat for barbecue lovers who like a big bite!

8 shark loin steaks (225g/8oz each)
100ml (3½fl oz) light soy sauce
100ml (3½fl oz) orange juice
50ml (2fl oz) ketchup
25g (1oz) freshly chopped parsley
2 tablespoons lime juice
2 garlic cloves minced
1 tablespoon ground black pepper

1. Mix the soy sauce, orange juice, ketchup, chopped parsley, lime juice, pepper and garlic.
2. Place the shark steaks into a zip-lock bag and pour the marinade over them.
3. Marinate in a refrigerator for 2 hours.
4. Grill the shark steaks over a hot barbecue for 6 minutes on each side.

GRILLED LOBSTER

Difficulty	Serves 2

A simple but tasty treat for fans of superb seafood.

1 large lobster halved
1 lemon cut into wedges
2 tablespoons olive oil
Herb butter (see recipe on page 164)

1. Using the blunt edge of a knife, crack the lobster claws and knuckles in two places on one side but take care to avoid crushing the meat.
2. Brush the shell and un-cracked side of the claws and knuckles with olive oil.
3. Place the lobster, cracked side up, on a plate and brush with herb butter.
4. Place the lobster, cracked side up, on the barbecue and cover with foil. Grill for 15 minutes, brushing occasionally with more herb butter.
5. Using tongs, check the lobster is done by pulling up the tail and checking the underside; it should be firm and dark orange.
6. Return the lobster to the grill if required but do not overcook, as it will become very tough.
7. When cooked, brush the tail with more herb butter and garnish with lemon wedges.

CHARGRILLED SOFT SHELL CRABS

Difficulty	Serves 4

A particular favourite in New Orleans, soft shell crabs have, as the name suggests, moulted recently and their new shell has yet to harden.

12 small soft shell crabs (usually available frozen)

1. Defrost and clean the crabs by removing the eyes and mouthparts.
2. Season with black pepper and place on a hot grill.
3. Cook for 5 minutes each side or until crisp and bright red.
4. Serve with your favourite fish sauce.

CEDAR WOOD SALMON

Difficulty	Serves 4

A superb alternative to expensive smoked salmon is this ingenious method of giving fish a subtle flavour of smoked cedar wood.

4 salmon steaks (240g/8oz, cut 3cm/1in thick)
100g (3½ oz) toasted sesame seeds (optional)
1 teaspoon grated lime rind
50ml (2fl oz) lime juice
1 tablespoon vegetable oil
1 teaspoon Dijon mustard
Pinch of pepper

1. Combine the lime rind and juice, oil, mustard and pepper together in a zip-lock bag.
2. Marinate salmon steaks at room temperature for 30 minutes, turning occasionally to coat each side evenly.
3. Remove the fish and sprinkle with sesame seeds.
4. Put the fish on to a sheet of cedar wood that's been soaked in water for 30 minutes.
5. Place the sheet on to a greased grill directly over a medium heat.
6. Grill for 16–20 minutes or until the fish flakes easily when pushed with a fork.

THAI SCALLOPS

Difficulty	Serves 4

Give your scallops an exotic oriental twist with this recipe from Mathew Shropshall, my friend and teammate in the Best of British BBQ team.

12 fresh scallops in their half-shells
3 finely chopped shallots
2 teaspoons Thai seasoning
1 lemon, grated rind and juice
2 finely chopped green chillies
2 finely chopped red chillies
Olive oil
Pinch of salt and pepper

1. Sprinkle all the ingredients evenly over the scallops.
2. Position a grill rack over the coals to heat.
3. Place the scallops in their half-shells on the grill and cook for 2–3 minutes.
4. Transfer on to a serving platter and enjoy.

FOIL-WRAPPED TROUT WITH LEMON AND DILL BUTTER

Difficulty 🍴🍴🍴	Serves 4

The traditional way for trout fishermen (and fisherwomen) to enjoy their catch.

4 fresh trout, cleaned and gutted
50ml (2fl oz) lemon juice
2 tablespoons butter
1 tablespoon chopped fresh parsley
1 teaspoon fresh dill
1 teaspoon salt
¼ teaspoon black pepper

1. Place each trout in the centre of a large foil square.
2. Melt the butter in a saucepan and add the lemon juice, parsley, dill, salt and pepper.
3. Stir and pour this mixture over the fish.
4. Fold the foil around each trout, sealing the edges.
5. Place on a medium-hot grill for 8–10 minutes.
6. Take care when opening the foil as the steam may scald.

Vegetarian and sides

Here are some great vegetarian options and delicious side dishes. They're healthy, easy to cook and the natural colours will brighten up your barbecue feast.

Vegetarian

With more and more people adopting a meat-free diet it makes sense to have a few tried and trusted vegetarian recipes in your barbecue repertoire.

GRILLED TOFU

Difficulty 🍴	Serves 4

Banish bland bean curd with this rice wine marinade from Japan.

500g (18oz) firm tofu
50ml (2fl oz) mirin rice wine
1 teaspoon fresh minced ginger
50ml (2fl oz) soy sauce
1 teaspoon cayenne pepper

1. Cut the tofu lengthwise into 4 portions.
2. Mix together the rice wine, ginger, soy sauce and cayenne pepper.
3. Marinate the tofu in the mixture for at least 1 hour in a zip-lock bag.
4. Grill the tofu over a high heat until heated through and lightly browned.

FLAT MUSHROOMS

Difficulty 🍴	Serves 4

Put the fun back into fungus with this sweet marinade for mushrooms.

8 large flat mushrooms
1 tablespoon olive oil
1 tablespoon light soy sauce
1 tablespoon crushed garlic
1 teaspoon chopped rosemary
1 teaspoon maple syrup
1 teaspoon sesame oil
Pinch of salt and black pepper

1. Rinse the mushrooms, remove and discard the stems.
2. Toss the mushrooms with the remaining ingredients and marinate for 5 minutes.
3. Grill the mushrooms until lightly charred and serve hot.

GRILLED ASPARAGUS WITH LEMON DIP

Difficulty	Serves 4

The English asparagus season is short (eight weeks beginning in late April/early May), but this delightful dip makes the wait worthwhile.

500g (18oz) asparagus
2 tablespoons olive oil
Pinch of salt and freshly ground pepper

LEMON DIP
25g (1oz) mayonnaise
1 teaspoon grated lemon rind
2 tablespoons lemon juice
Pinch of freshly ground pepper

1. Preheat the grill to high.
2. Discard the coarse woody ends of the asparagus stalks.
3. Brush oil on the asparagus and place across the grill.
4. Cook for 2–3 minutes per side or until crisp and tender.
5. Season with salt and pepper.
6. To make the lemon dip combine all the ingredients and season to taste.

SPICY BEAN BURGERS

Difficulty	Serves 8

Mexican salsa and fiery chilli powder spice up this vegetarian version of the All-American hamburger.

800g (1¾lb) tinned kidney beans
2 tablespoons salsa
100g (3½oz) breadcrumbs
25g (1oz) freshly chopped coriander
4 teaspoons chilli powder
1 medium egg
2 tablespoons olive oil

1. Wash and drain the beans then blend in a food processer.
2. Mix in the salsa, breadcrumbs, coriander, chilli powder and egg.
3. Using your hands, mould the mix into 8 burger shapes.
4. Brush each burger with olive oil and grill on a medium-hot heat for 5 minutes on each side until golden.

Salads and slaws

Forget limp lettuce and tired tomatoes, these salads will add plenty of crunchy interest to your barbecues.

COLESLAW WITH APPLE

Difficulty	Serves 8

Try this take on the cabbage-based classic with pork chops or pork burgers to really release the apple flavours.

400g (14oz) shredded red cabbage
8 apples, peeled, cored and thinly sliced
100ml (3½fl oz) sour cream
100ml (3½fl oz) mayonnaise
1 tablespoon lemon juice
1 teaspoon celery salt
1 teaspoon sugar
Pinch of ground black pepper

1. Mix the sour cream, mayonnaise, lemon juice, celery salt, sugar and pepper in a large bowl.
2. Add the cabbage and apple slices and toss lightly until the cabbage is coated.

RED SLAW

Difficulty	Serves 8

If you thought cabbage was only fit for pet tortoises, this terrific tangy dressing will change your mind.

1 whole shredded red cabbage
200ml (7fl oz) tomato purée
1 teaspoon lipsmackin' barbecue sauce (see recipe on page 169)
1 tablespoon English mustard
1 teaspoon Tabasco
1 teaspoon Worcestershire sauce
100ml (3½fl oz) mayonnaise
1 tablespoon sugar
3 tablespoons vinegar
½ tablespoon salt
½ tablespoon pepper

1. Combine all the ingredients in a bowl.
2. Chill before serving.

HONEY AND MUSTARD POTATO SALAD

Difficulty		Serves 8

Honey and mustard aren't just perfect partners for ham, they can give a real zing to the humble spud too.

5 large chopped potatoes
250ml (9fl oz) mayonnaise
2 chopped hard boiled eggs
120ml (4fl oz) American yellow mustard
50ml (1fl oz) honey
50ml (1fl oz) white wine vinegar
25g (1 oz) finely chopped chives
1 tablespoon horseradish
Pinch of salt and ground black pepper

1. Boil the potatoes in a saucepan for 15 minutes. Drain the water and gently add the vinegar, garlic, onion, eggs, chives, and mustard.
2. Mix together the mayonnaise, honey, horseradish, salt and black pepper in a small mixing bowl.
3. Pour this mixture over the potatoes and gently coat.
4. Allow the potato salad to cool before serving.

GRILLED BACON AND POTATO SALAD

Difficulty		Serves 4

No American picnic would be complete without potato salad and this recipe is sure to satisfy.

4 medium-sized potatoes
2 tablespoons olive oil
4 slices thick-cut bacon
2 tablespoons cider vinegar
25g (1oz) chopped flat-leaf parsley
Pinch of ground black pepper and salt

1. Scrub the potatoes clean and cut into 1.5cm (½in) slices. Brush with olive oil and sprinkle with salt.
2. Place potato slices and bacon slices on a medium grill and cook until the bacon releases easily.
3. Turn the bacon and cook until the bacon is starting to brown and the potatoes are grill-marked.
4. Remove the bacon and turn the potatoes over and cook until tender.
5. Chop the bacon and cut the potatoes into bite-size pieces and place in a medium bowl.
6. Add the cider vinegar and parsley and serve warm.

Breads and pizzas

To accompany your meal, add one of these tasty flavoursome breads or make your own hand-finished pizza.

HOME-MADE CARDAMOM NAAN BREAD

Difficulty /////   **Serves 8**

This beautiful bread from the Indian sub-continent can also be baked on your back garden barbecue.

2 teaspoons active dry yeast
250ml (9fl oz) lukewarm water (40°C/104°F)
1 tablespoon honey
1 tablespoon extra virgin olive oil
400g (14oz) bread flour
1 tablespoon salt
1 tablespoon ground cardamom

1. In a large bowl, dissolve the yeast in the water and stir in the honey.
2. Let this stand for about 10 minutes until foamy.
3. Add the oil, flour, salt and cardamom then stir until the dough forms a cohesive mass.
4. Turn the dough out on to a lightly floured surface and knead for about 6 minutes until smooth and elastic.
5. Divide the dough into 8 pieces and shape each piece into a ball.
6. Set the balls on an oiled baking sheet, brush with oil and cover loosely with cling film.
7. Put the dough balls in a warm place until they've doubled in bulk. This should take between 1 and 2 hours but the dough can be refrigerated overnight if you push down the balls before chilling.
8. On a lightly floured surface, roll out each ball into a 20cm (8in) disc.
9. Arrange them on 3 oiled baking sheets and let them rest for 20 minutes.
10. Prepare the barbecue on a medium-high heat.
11. Brush each naan lightly with olive oil and grill for about 1 minute, until golden on the bottom and light bubbles form on the top.
12. Turn and cook for about 1 minute until golden all over. Keep the cooked naan breads warm while you bake the others.

HOME-MADE PIZZA ON THE BARBECUE

Difficulty /////   **Serves 4**

Even without a proper wood-fired oven you can still bake perfect pizza with this recipe designed for any gas or charcoal grill.

DOUGH
1 teaspoon salt
120ml (4fl oz) warm water
2 teaspoons light brown sugar
2 sachets fast action dried yeast (7g/¼oz)
750g (1½lb) white flour
50g (2oz) corn meal cornflour
25g (1oz) whole wheat flour
4 tablespoons olive oil

SAUCE
4 garlic cloves minced
50ml (2fl oz) whipping cream
3 tablespoons freshly chopped basil
3 tablespoons freshly chopped oregano
8 ripe plum tomatoes, peeled, seeded and chopped
3 tablespoons unsalted butter
1 teaspoon salt

TOPPING
Olive oil
Crumbled gorgonzola cheese (or similar)
Any other ingredient you like!

1. Measure 60ml (just over 2fl oz) of warm water in a bowl, add the sugar and yeast and stir to dissolve.
2. Stand for at least 5 minutes to 'proof' (froth forms on top).
3. Sift the white flour, wheat flour, corn meal and salt into a bowl.
4. Make a depression in the middle of the flour and add 3 tablespoons of olive oil and 60ml of warm water.
5. Add the yeast mixture and mix all ingredients with your hands. Gather the dough and place it on a pre-floured board.
6. Knead the dough for 10 minutes to form a smooth, elastic mass, adding more flour if the dough is too sticky.
7. Grease a large bowl with olive oil and add the dough, turning it to coat the top.
8. Cover and let it rise in a warm place until doubled in size (approximately 45 minutes).
9. Make the sauce by melting the butter in a pan.
10. Add the garlic and sweat for one minute.
11. Add the tomatoes and cook for 2 minutes, stirring constantly.
12. Add the cream, basil and oregano and bring to the boil.
13. Once the dough has risen divide into 6 equal pieces.

14. On a floured surface, roll out the dough into a round shape about 1.5cm (½in) thick.
15. Coat both sides of the shaped crust with olive oil.
16. Place directly on a hot clean grill until the upper surface begins to bubble (about 2 minutes).
17. Watch the crust closely and rotate with a spatula if necessary.
18. Remove the crust and turn cooked side up (it should be golden brown).
19. Brush with olive oil, sauce, cheese and your desired toppings.
20. Sprinkle some olive oil over each pizza.
21. Return for final cooking (2–4 minutes), rotating for even cooking.

BEER BREAD

Difficulty		Serves 4

A quick and easy bread to bake on your barbecue.

300g (10½oz) self-raising flour
2 tablespoons sugar
1 can stout beer at room temperature
Pinch of salt

1. Mix all ingredients together in a bowl.
2. When everything is well mixed and runny, pour into a greased loaf tin and place on a medium heat for about 15 minutes.

GARLIC BREAD

Difficulty		Serves 6

You could buy 'heat and eat' garlic bread from a supermarket, but making your own is much more satisfying and tastes better too.

1 loaf French bread
¾ teaspoon garlic powder or 2 garlic cloves finely chopped
100g (3½oz) softened butter

1. Slice the bread but do not cut through the bottom crust.
2. Add the garlic to the butter and blend thoroughly.
3. Spread between the slices and over top of the bread.
4. Wrap in aluminium foil and seal the edges.
5. Heat on a low heat on the back of the grill for 10–15 minutes.
6. Serve hot.

GRILLED TUSCAN BREAD

Difficulty		Serves 4

Recall lazy summer days in Tuscany with this tasty bread topping.

4 large ripe tomatoes
25g (1oz) torn basil leaves
6 slices of country-style bread, cut in half
3 garlic cloves lightly crushed
Pinch of salt and pepper
4 tablespoons olive oil

1. Wash the tomatoes and cut in half. Remove as many seeds as possible and dice. Put the pieces in a small bowl and combine with the basil.
2. Grill the bread slices and turn so that both sides are light brown.
3. Rub each slice with a garlic clove.
4. Spoon some of the tomato mixture over the bread, sprinkle with the salt and pepper and drizzle with olive oil.

Potatoes and vegetables

Besides the cold salads mentioned earlier, try these recipes for cooked vegetables which can work equally well as starters, sides or even as vegetarian main courses.

BAKED POTATOES

Difficulty 🍴	Serves 4

No Guy Fawkes Night would be complete without potatoes baking in the bonfire's embers, but you can also enjoy this recipe all year round.

4 medium-sized baking potatoes
2 tablespoons olive oil

1. Wash the potatoes, scrub to remove any black spots and prick the skin a few times with a fork.
2. Rub the olive oil all over the potato (you can also add seasoning to give a flavour to the skin).
3. Wrap the potatoes in foil and cook over a low-medium heat for 45 minutes (depending on size), ensuring you rotate the potato throughout cooking.
4. Serve with a choice of fillings such as grated cheese or baked beans.

SWEET POTATO WEDGES

Difficulty 🍴	Serves 4

This recipe is inspired by my oldest friend Tobie Holbrook who introduced me to the creamy, sweet and spicy flavour of sweet potatoes.

1kg (2.2lb) medium sweet potatoes, cut lengthwise
    into 6 wedges
2 tablespoons olive oil
Pinch of salt and pepper
Pinch of cayenne pepper

1. Boil the potatoes in a saucepan for 5 minutes until slightly soft.
2. Drain the water and put the potatoes into a bowl. Then toss with the olive oil, salt, pepper and cayenne.
3. Grill over a medium heat for about 15 minutes, turning until lightly charred.

POTATO HALVES

Difficulty		Serves 4

You've never tasted tastier potatoes than these superior spuds.

4 russet potatoes
2 garlic cloves
¼ teaspoon salt
2 tablespoons olive oil
½ teaspoon dried oregano
Pinch of pepper

1. Scrub the potatoes and cut in half lengthwise.
2. Purée the garlic and transfer to a small bowl. Add the salt, oil and oregano and blend well.
3. Add a pinch of pepper to taste and leave to stand for at least 10 minutes.
4. Cook the potatoes in boiling water for about 15 minutes until just tender.
5. Drain and brush with seasoned oil.
6. Grill on a medium heat, turning and brushing with oil occasionally, for about 15 minutes until slightly charred on all surfaces.

CORN ON THE COB

Difficulty		Serves 8

Use coriander, chilli powder and cumin to turn everyday corn on the cob into an award-winning side dish.

8 corn on the cobs
6 tablespoons soft butter
1 tablespoon chopped coriander
¼ teaspoon chilli powder
½ teaspoon ground cumin

1. Combine the butter, coriander, chilli powder and cumin.
2. Rub the ears of corn evenly with the mixture.
3. Preheat the grill to medium-high and grill the corn for 15 minutes, turning occasionally.

ESCALIBADA (GRILLED CATALAN VEGETABLES)

Difficulty	Serves 4

A smoky flavour is the key ingredient in this speciality of Barcelona.

2 red bell peppers
2 green or yellow bell peppers
2 medium aubergines
4 medium tomatoes
2 medium courgettes
8 button mushrooms

DRESSING
1 tablespoon chopped parsley
50ml (2fl oz) olive oil
2 tablespoons vinegar
1 garlic clove diced

1. Grill the peppers and courgettes over a moderate heat on the barbecue.
2. Pierce the skin of the aubergines to prevent them from bursting and grill them with the peppers for 15 minutes, turning several times.
3. When the skins are blistered and charred remove from the heat.
4. Wrap in a towel, place in a paper bag and set aside.
5. Score each of the tomato skins with a cross and grill with the mushrooms for 5 minutes, turning occasionally.
6. When cool, peel the peppers and aubergines and remove the pepper seeds.
7. Peel the tomatoes, slice the vegetables and arrange them on a platter with the tomatoes in the middle.
8. Toss the dressing ingredients and drizzle over the vegetables.

CHARRED SWEET PEPPERS

Difficulty	Serves 4

Perfect peppers with a tasty twist.

4 tablespoons red wine vinegar
1 tablespoon Dijon mustard
2 tablespoons finely chopped red onion
4 garlic cloves finely chopped
2 large red bell peppers quartered
2 large green bell peppers quartered
Pinch of pepper

1. Combine the mustard, onion, garlic and pepper in a bowl.
2. Place the peppers on the grill and brush with the mustard mixture.
3. Cook until lightly charred and then turn.
4. Brush the other side and cook until browned and slightly softened.

GRILLED AUBERGINE

Difficulty	Serves 6

This simple seasoning will transform ordinary eggplant into something extra-special.

1 large aubergine
50g (2oz) melted butter
½ teaspoon garlic salt
½ teaspoon Italian seasoning
¼ teaspoon salt
Pinch of pepper

1. Peel the aubergine and cut into 2cm (¾in) thick slices.
2. Combine the butter, garlic salt and Italian seasoning and stir well.
3. Brush the aubergine slices with the butter mixture and sprinkle with salt and pepper.
4. Grill over a medium heat for 10 minutes or until tender, turning and basting occasionally with the butter mixture.

BBQ BEANS

Difficulty	Serves 12

Thanks to my great friend Gareth Williams for this terrifically tasty version of the classic cowboy side dish.

4 tins baked beans
4 slices diced bacon
50g chopped onion
1 tablespoon general rub (see recipe on page 164)
300ml (10½fl oz) gold plated barbecue sauce (see recipe on page 166)
50g (2oz) brown sugar

1. Use a barbecue skillet to fry the bacon until crispy. Add the onion and cook until soft.
2. Transfer the bacon to a saucepan and add the beans, rub, sauce and brown sugar.
3. Simmer for 20 minutes and serve.

Puddings and desserts

Yes, you can cook puddings and desserts on a barbecue, even (believe it or not) ice cream!

CALYPSO GRILLED PINEAPPLE

Difficulty   **Serves 8**

A welcome surprise for anyone who thought pineapple could only be served with gammon.

100ml (3½fl oz) Worcestershire sauce
100ml (3½fl oz) honey
100g (3½oz) butter
100g (3½oz) light brown sugar
100ml (3½fl oz) dark rum
1 pineapple cut into 8 wedges
1 tub vanilla ice cream

1. Combine the Worcestershire sauce, honey, butter, sugar and rum in a saucepan.
2. Bring to a full boil over medium-high heat, stirring frequently.
3. Reduce the heat to medium-low and simmer for 10 minutes, or until the sauce is slightly thickened, stirring frequently.
4. Remove from the heat and allow to cool completely.
5. Brush the pineapple wedges with some of the sauce and place them on an oiled grill.
6. Cook on a high heat for 5 minutes or until glazed, turning and basting frequently with the sauce.
7. Serve with ice cream and the remaining sauce.

BANANAS FOSTER

Difficulty   **Serves 4**

Named after a New Orleans restaurateur's best friend, this is a true taste of 'The Big Easy'.

50g (2oz) butter
100g (3½oz) brown sugar
½ teaspoon cinnamon
25ml (1fl oz) Crème de banane liqueur
4 bananas cut in half lengthways, then halved
25ml (1fl oz) dark rum
4 scoops vanilla ice cream

1. Put the butter, sugar and cinnamon in a saucepan.
2. Place over a low heat and stir until the sugar dissolves.
3. Add the banana liqueur and place the bananas in the pan.
4. When the banana sections soften and begin to brown carefully add the rum.
5. Continue to cook the sauce until the rum is hot and then tip the pan slightly to ignite the rum.
6. Let the flames subside and lift the bananas out of the pan.
7. Place 4 pieces over a portion of ice cream.
8. Spoon warm sauce generously over the top of the ice cream and serve immediately.

GRILLED PEACHES WITH RASPBERRY SAUCE

Difficulty 🍴🍴🍴 **Serves 4**

Scottish raspberries and Georgia peaches make an unusual combination but a delicious dessert.

150g (5oz) frozen raspberries in syrup, slightly thawed
2 teaspoons lemon juice
2 fresh peeled and halved peaches
25g (1oz) brown sugar
1 teaspoon ground cinnamon
½ teaspoon vanilla extract
1 teaspoon butter

1. Use a food processor or blender to process the raspberries and lemon juice until puréed.
2. Using a sieve, strain the liquid and discard the seeds. Cover and chill.
3. Place the peach halves, cut side up, on to a large piece of foil.
4. Combine the brown sugar and cinnamon and sprinkle into peach centres.
5. Sprinkle with the vanilla and dot with the butter.
6. Fold the foil over the peaches and seal.
7. Grill the foil parcel over a medium hot barbecue for 12–15 minutes.
8. To serve, spoon the raspberry sauce over the peaches.

ORANGE EGG CUSTARD

Difficulty 🍴🍴 **Serves 1**

A tangy tropical twist for a classic English custard.

1 orange
1 large egg
2 tablespoons milk
1 tablespoon sugar

1. Slice the top off the orange and remove all the fruit pulp, but save the empty skin to use as an 'orange cup'.
2. Crack an egg into a bowl and add the milk and sugar.
3. Gently whisk with a fork, but don't over-mix – you want the lumps of smooth egg white when it's cooked.
4. Place the egg mixture in the orange cup and place them over a grilling stand over a low heat.
5. Cook for 20–30 minutes but wait until the egg looks cooked but not hard.

GRILLED BANANAS WITH IRISH CREAM LIQUEUR

Difficulty 🍴 **Serves 4**

A truly exotic combination of tropical fruit and Irish charm.

8 good-sized bananas
Irish cream liqueur

1. Wrap the unpeeled bananas in foil and barbecue for 15 minutes, turning once, until the bananas are soft.
2. Slit along the top lengthways and pour the Irish cream liqueur over them.

BARBECUED BAKED ALASKA

Difficulty	Serves 4

You don't need to be a magician to barbecue ice cream but this dramatic dessert is sure to impress your guests!

4 individual sponge cakes
4 scoops ice cream
3 egg whites
¼ teaspoon cream of tartar
6 tablespoons sugar
½ teaspoon vinegar

1. Cut each sponge cake in half and sandwich a scoop of ice cream between them.
2. Put these into the freezer until they're frozen firm.
3. Beat the cream of tartar and egg whites until they're frothy.
4. Gradually add the sugar and continue beating until they're stiff and shiny. Stir in the vinegar.
5. Cover each cake sandwich with the meringue mixture.
6. Seal the edges at the bottom and cover each cake evenly then put them back in the freezer until everyone is ready for dessert.
7. Barbecue the dessert shells on a medium-low heat for between 3 and 5 minutes.
8. Serve immediately the meringue is nicely browned.
9. You may also brown the top with a blowtorch and add a decorative sparkler if you like!

Top Tip

Turn your marshmallows into 'smores' (some-mores) by serving them with a smoky bourbon and chocolate sauce sandwiched between two Graham (digestive) biscuits. Invented in 1927, smores are the signature dish of the American Girl Scout Association!

TOASTED HOME-MADE MARSHMALLOWS

Difficulty	Serves 10

You can't have a campfire without toasting marshmallows and they'll taste even better if you've made them yourself.

Spray oil
Icing sugar
20g (¾oz) leaf gelatine
250ml (9fl oz) water
300g (10½oz) sugar
200ml (7fl oz) glucose-fructose syrup (or corn syrup)
¼ teaspoon salt
2 teaspoons vanilla essence

1. Coat a 28 x 35cm (11 x 14in) pan (at least 5cm/2in deep) with spray oil.
2. Heavily dust the pan with icing sugar.
3. Mix the gelatine with 120ml (4fl oz) of the water and let stand for 25 minutes.
4. In a saucepan with a thick bottom, combine the remaining water, sugar, glucose-fructose syrup and salt.
5. Heat over a low to medium heat until the sugar has dissolved.
6. Increase the heat to high and boil whilst stirring constantly.
7. Once boiled reduce the heat to medium and simmer for 15 minutes, stirring constantly.
8. Place the gelatine mixture in a food processor and with the whisk attachment on low power slowly pour in the hot sugar mixture.
9. Increase the whisk to high and beat for 15 minutes. The mixture should become thick, white and nearly tripled in volume.
10. Add the vanilla essence and 1 tablespoon of water and beat until combined.
11. Spoon the mixture into the prepared pan and leave to stand uncovered overnight.
12. Loosen the mixture from the pan by running a hot knife around the edges.
13. Turn the pan upside down on to a board dusted with icing sugar.
14. With a large knife, cut the block of marshmallow into 2.5cm (1in) squares and sprinkle with icing sugar or desiccated coconut.
15. Place a square on to a wooden skewer and toast over a medium barbecue.

Essential extras

Turn your barbecue into a great barbecue with these tried and tested extras that will make your food look interesting as well as taste interesting.

Rubs, marinades and sauces

Salsas, dips, dressings and relishes

Rubs, marinades and sauces

Besides the best cuts of meat, poultry and fish the essential tools for any expert barbecuer are a selection of classic rubs, marinades and sauces. Half the fun of grilling is experimenting and creating your own variations of lipsmackin' BBQ sauce, rib rubs and raspberry marinade but here are my favourite recipes to get you started...

HERB BUTTER RUB

Difficulty

A simple seasoning that's a must for many barbecue dishes.

4 tablespoons softened butter
2 tablespoons finely chopped parsley
2 tablespoons finely chopped chives
1 teaspoon lemon juice
Pinch of salt and pepper

Combine all the ingredients with a fork and apply during cooking.

GENERAL RUB FOR MEAT, POULTRY AND SEAFOOD

Difficulty

An easy-to-make multipurpose rub that will take any roasted or grilled barbecue dish to the next level.

50g (2oz) salt
1 tablespoon garlic powder
1 tablespoon freshly ground black pepper
1 tablespoon paprika
1 teaspoon powdered onion
¼ teaspoon cayenne pepper
¼ teaspoon dried thyme
¼ teaspoon dried oregano

Mix all of the ingredients together, store in a glass jar and use as required.

GENERAL RIB RUB

Difficulty

This simple rub is a real rib tickler.

2 tablespoons white sugar
1 tablespoon light brown sugar
2 tablespoons smoked Hungarian paprika
2 tablespoons celery salt
1½ teaspoons chilli powder
1½ teaspoons ground cumin
1 teaspoon onion powder
1 teaspoon white pepper
1 teaspoon finely ground black pepper

1. **Combine the sugars, paprika, salt, chilli powder, cumin, onion powder and peppers and mix well.**
2. **Place the rub in an airtight container and store in a dark cupboard until ready to use.**

GENERAL PORK RUB

Difficulty

Whether it's chops, steaks or ribs, don't barbecue pork without this remarkably versatile rub.

8 tablespoons smoked paprika
4 teaspoons onion powder
4 teaspoons garlic powder
2 teaspoons cumin
4 teaspoons black pepper
1 teaspoon cayenne pepper
4 teaspoons celery salt

Combine all the ingredients, store in an airtight jar and use as required.

TERIYAKI MARINADE

Difficulty	Serves 4

The great glaze of Japan will bring a touch of the mysterious east to any British barbecue.

250ml (9fl oz) Teriyaki sauce
50ml (2fl oz) pineapple juice
50g (2oz) chilli flakes
50g (2oz) minced garlic
50g (2oz) diced onion
50g (2oz) brown sugar
1 tablespoon ground black pepper

Combine all the ingredients and store for one week before using.

KETCHUP

Difficulty	Serves 20

Whether it's ketchup, catsup or tomato sauce, no burger is complete without it.

2kg (4½lb) ripe tomatoes
100ml (3½fl oz) white vinegar
2 tablespoons salt
50g (2oz) sugar
2 garlic cloves
100g (3½oz) onion
1 tablespoon black peppercorns
¼ teaspoon ground allspice
¼ teaspoon cinnamon
¼ teaspoon cayenne pepper
½ teaspoon ground ginger
½ teaspoon garlic powder
6 cloves

1. Remove the core and chop the tomatoes before placing them in a large saucepan.
2. Add the vinegar and salt and bring to the boil and cook for 5 minutes, crushing with a hand masher.
3. Purée using a hand blender or food processor.
4. Add all the remaining ingredients to the liquid and simmer for 30 minutes until syrupy.
5. Let the ketchup cool and store in airtight jars.

SATAY SAUCE

Difficulty		Serves 10

Try this recipe for the signature sauce of South-East Asia.

250ml (9fl oz) coconut cream
70g (2½oz) peanut butter
2 teaspoons Worcestershire sauce
2 teaspoons chilli powder
2 teaspoons Madras curry powder
1 lime, grated rind and juice

1. Pour the coconut cream into a saucepan and heat.
2. Add the peanut butter and stir until blended.
3. Add the Worcestershire sauce, lime juice, rind and spices and heat gently for 4–5 minutes.

Top tip!

This sauce also makes a good dip.

TOMATO AND STRAWBERRY GLAZE

Difficulty		Serves 20

Another unusual combination, but try it – I think you'll like it.

1 litre (1¾ pints) cider vinegar
1kg (2.2lb) jam sugar
1kg (2.2lb) vine tomatoes
500g (18oz) strawberries
Fresh mint leaves

1. Put the tomatoes into a saucepan of hot water and simmer for 5 minutes until the skins begin to peel off.
2. Drain the water, remove the skins and core and chop the flesh into quarters.
3. Hull the strawberries and quarter.
4. Use a thick-bottomed saucepan to melt the sugar in the vinegar over a low heat.
5. Once dissolved add the strawberries and tomatoes and boil on a high heat for 20 minutes.
6. Cool for 1 hour and blend in several mint leaves.
7. Store in an airtight container and leave for 2 weeks to mature before using.

BEEF MARINADE

Difficulty		Serves 4

Something no back garden barbecuer should be without is a good marinade for beef – try this tasty recipe on your next steak or kebab.

1 teaspoon dry mustard
1 teaspoon ground cumin
1 crumbled bay leaf
1 garlic clove minced
250ml (9fl oz) beef stock
50ml (2fl oz) Worcestershire sauce
1 tablespoon cider vinegar
1 tablespoon vegetable oil
1 teaspoon hot pepper sauce

1. Blend the mustard, cumin, bay leaf and garlic in a plastic jug.
2. Boil the beef stock, pour the mixture and mix well.
3. Stir in the Worcestershire sauce, vinegar, oil and pepper sauce.
4. Cover and cool (any leftover marinade can be frozen and reused).

GOLD PLATED BARBECUE SAUCE

Difficulty		Serves 8

Another classic American condiment, this time inspired by the vinegar-based sauces of the Carolinas.

200g (7oz) sugar
16 tablespoons cornflour
4 teaspoons allspice
4 teaspoons ground cloves
1 litre (1¾ pints) fresh orange juice
16 tablespoons vinegar
32 tablespoons butter

1. Combine the sugar, cornflour, allspice and cloves in a saucepan.
2. Slowly stir in the orange juice and vinegar.
3. Stir constantly over a medium heat until the sauce thickens.
4. Boil for 3 minutes and stir in the butter.

RASPBERRY MARINADE

Difficulty 🍴	Serves 6

A fantastic sweet'n'sour fruit marinade that's a perfect partner for many meats.

500g (18oz) fresh raspberries
200ml (7fl oz) raspberry vinegar
50ml (2fl oz) olive oil
2 bay leaves
1 tablespoon dried thyme

1. Combine the raspberries and vinegar in a saucepan, heat to boiling and boil for 1 minute.
2. Remove from the heat and stir in the oil, bay leaves and thyme.
3. Cool to room temperature before use.

LIPSMACKIN' BARBECUE SAUCE

Difficulty 🍴🍴	Serves 8

Every great griller has their own recipe for lipsmackin' BBQ sauce and here's mine, inspired by the sweet tomato-based signature sauces of Memphis and Kansas City.

250ml (9fl oz) ketchup
200g (7oz) powdered sugar
1 tablespoon Worcestershire sauce
6 tablespoons molasses
¼ teaspoon garlic salt
½ teaspoon liquid barbecue smoke

1. Mix all the ingredients in a saucepan.
2. Stir over a medium heat until boiling.
3. Simmer on a low heat for 10–15 minutes until the sauce has thickened.

CHILLI AND LIME SAUCE

Difficulty 🍴🍴	Serves 6

A spicy hot sauce featuring the fiery 'mountain' chillies of Mexico called Serrano.

3 small green finely chopped Serrano chillies
3 garlic cloves
2 tablespoons fresh coriander leaves
1 teaspoon sugar
¼ teaspoon salt
100ml (3½fl oz) fresh lime juice
50ml (2fl oz) chicken stock

1. Use a pestle and mortar to pound the chillies, garlic, coriander leaves, sugar and salt into a smooth paste.
2. Put the chilli mixture into a saucepan with the lime juice and stock and bring to the boil.

CHIMICHURRI SAUCE

Difficulty 🍴🍴	Serves 6

Here's a recipe for the signature sauce of South America which, legend has it, was invented by a British meat importer named Jimmy Curry.

4 jalapeno peppers finely chopped and de-seeded
50g (2oz) chopped onion
4 garlic cloves chopped
25g (1oz) freshly chopped parsley
1 teaspoon oregano
1 teaspoon fresh ground black pepper
100ml (3½fl oz) olive oil
50ml (2fl oz) red wine vinegar
2 tablespoons lemon juice
50ml (2fl oz) water

Combine all the ingredients – that's all there is to it!

SMOKY BOURBON CHOCOLATE SAUCE

Difficulty 🍴🍴	Serves 8

Great with toasted marshmallows, but leave out the whiskey if cooking it for kids.

150ml (5fl oz) whipping cream
2 tablespoons dark brown sugar
150g (5oz) dark chocolate
1 tablespoon bourbon whiskey
1 teaspoon vanilla essence

1. In a saucepan over a medium heat, combine the cream and brown sugar.
2. Stir until the sugar dissolves and the cream just starts to boil.
3. Take off the heat, add the chocolate and stir until smooth.
4. Stir in the bourbon whiskey and vanilla essence.

Salsas, dips, dressings and relishes

The finishing touch for any salad or side dish is a superb salsa, relish, dip or dressing.

PINEAPPLE SALSA

Difficulty		Serves 8

Hawaii meets Mexico in this Pacific Coast classic.

½ medium red bell pepper, finely diced
200g (7oz) fresh pineapple cubes
50ml (2fl oz) pineapple juice
50g (2oz) thinly sliced onion
2 tablespoons fresh chopped coriander
2 tablespoons fresh chopped parsley

In a medium-sized bowl, stir together all the ingredients and season with salt and ground black pepper.

CUCUMBER AND MINT DIP

Difficulty		Serves 8

An English dip that's quite delightful on a summer's day.

½ cucumber, coarsely grated
20g (¾oz) freshly chopped mint leaves
300g (10½oz) natural yoghurt
Pinch of salt and pepper

Mix the yogurt, mint and cucumber in a bowl and season to taste.

MAYONNAISE AND PESTO DIP

Difficulty		Serves 2

An inspired Italian dip – try it spread on fresh focaccia.

2 tablespoons basil pesto
2 tablespoons mayonnaise
2 tablespoons finely chopped black olives
A squeeze of lemon juice

Fold all the ingredients together and chill before serving.

GRILLED PEACH SALSA

Difficulty		Serves 2

A light and fruity salsa, try it on your favourite burger with a glass of Pinot Grigio white wine.

4–6 fresh peach halves, pitted and peeled
1 tablespoon olive oil
1 tablespoon lemon juice
1 finely chopped red onion
Sprig of chopped mint
Pinch of salt

1. Brush the peach halves with some olive oil and add a pinch of salt.
2. Grill over a medium heat for about 2 minutes per side.
3. Cool and dice the peaches and mix with the lemon juice, red onion and mint.

CHIPOTLE HONEY SALSA

Difficulty		Serves 4

A fantastic salsa featuring the smoked jalapeno chilli peppers that are an essential ingredient of the best Tex-Mex barbecues.

4 teaspoons chipotle paste
100ml (3½fl oz) water
1 can tomato paste (170g/6oz)
150ml (5fl oz) honey
1 bunch chopped coriander
1 tablespoon fresh lime juice

1. Use a food processor or blender to combine all the ingredients until smooth.
2. Serve chilled.

Top tip!
The salsa will also keep for one week in a refrigerator.

TOMATO AND LIME DRESSING

Difficulty	Serves 8

A wonderfully refreshing and highly versatile dressing that's perfect for a summer's day.

3 peeled, seeded and chopped tomatoes
3 chopped shallots
50ml (2fl oz) sherry wine vinegar
50ml (2fl oz) tomato juice
50ml (2fl oz) extra virgin olive oil
1 juiced lime
2 tablespoons fresh chopped parsley
2 tablespoons fresh chopped coriander
2 tablespoons fresh chopped basil
Combine all the ingredients and serve.

RASPBERRY DRESSING

Difficulty	Serves 20

A superb Scottish salad dressing that's best when made with the finest Blairgowrie raspberries.

200g (7oz) fresh raspberries
200ml (7fl oz) raspberry vinegar
200ml (7fl oz) extra virgin olive oil
200ml (7fl oz) rapeseed oil
200ml (7fl oz) maple syrup
1 tablespoon Dijon mustard
1 tablespoon freshly chopped tarragon
1 teaspoon salt
Combine all the ingredients in a food processor or whisk vigorously until the dressing thickens and is well blended.

CITRUS VINAIGRETTE

Difficulty	Serves 2

A simple citrus dressing that will add zest to any summer salad.

2 tablespoons orange juice
2 tablespoons grapefruit juice
2 tablespoons lime juice
2 tablespoons honey
2 tablespoons Dijon mustard
Whisk all the ingredients in a mixing bowl to dissolve the honey.

SWEET CORN RELISH

Difficulty	Serves 10

A sweet and spicy relish that will make any burger fit for a jolly green giant!

400g (14oz) tinned sweet corn
2 de-seeded and diced red peppers
2 finely diced celery sticks
1 de-seeded and diced red chill
1 diced white onion
400ml (14fl oz) white wine vinegar
200g (7fl oz) caster sugar
2 teaspoons salt
2 teaspoons mustard powder
½ teaspoon ground turmeric

1. Drain the sweet corn and discard the liquid. Put all the ingredients in a saucepan and bring to the boil.
2. Reduce the heat and simmer gently for 20 minutes, constantly stirring.
3. Allow to cool and store in airtight jars until needed.

VINE-RIPENED TOMATO RELISH

Difficulty	Serves 4

A premier relish that relies on using the best tomatoes for its success.

1 tablespoon olive oil
1 chopped onion
2 garlic cloves chopped
150g (5oz) crushed vine-ripened tomatoes
30g (1½oz) chopped sun-dried tomatoes
2 tablespoons tomato purée
2 tablespoons honey
2 tablespoons chopped fresh lemon thyme
Pinch of salt and pepper

1. Heat the oil in a frying pan and add the onion and garlic until lightly browned.
2. Add the rest of the ingredients and simmer for 15 minutes until reduced and thickened.
3. Season with salt and pepper.

COMPETITIONS
GLOSSARY
USEFUL CONTACTS
INDEX

The next level: competing in barbecue contests

There's only one thing more satisfying than creating your own recipes and using them successfully on your own back garden grill, and that's winning a contest for cooking the best barbecue beef, chicken or pork!

Whatever we do, there's something deep inside us that wants to test our talents in some form of contest, and barbecuing is no exception. In America there are now more than 500 major contests held from coast to coast, and I've been lucky enough to compete at some of the most famous. They include the Jack Daniel's World Championship Invitational, held in Lynchburg, Tennessee, where I won the 'I Know Jack…About Grilling' category, and the American Royal World Series team event, held annually in Kansas City, which attracts over 500 entries every year.

Naturally, travelling thousands of miles to cook takes weeks of planning and preparation. Just packing a suitcase is a challenge since half of the 23kg/50lb baggage allowance is always taken up with rubs and sauces! Beside packing, the list of things that need organising includes entry forms, flights, car hire, hotels, visas, shopping lists, team clothing, chefs' jackets and even 'compliance with local hygiene declarations', but all the hard work is definitely worth it – whatever the final result.

I'm delighted to say that the competitive barbecuing community is fantastically friendly and I'm very grateful to the sponsors, teams and contest organisers that have loaned me equipment over the years.

One particular example of kindness, that went above and beyond the call of duty, came at the I Love Barbecue Festival held at Lake Placid in New York State, when Mark Grimmette, a KCBS (Kansas City Barbecue Society) judge and double Olympic luge champion, drove 150 miles to lend us his char-griller.

American barbecue contests are quite unlike similar culinary competitions in the UK. This is because US cook-offs are often the main reason for the event rather than a sideshow attached to a village fete or country fair. Many contests also raise money for charity and include a full weekend of live entertainment for competitors and spectators alike. Some teams are now semi-professional and compete every weekend for the prize money, and the all-important bragging rights, available in each category.

Most American barbecue contests are for smoker-style barbecues, and a typical team event will see each group allocated a 20ft x 20ft space in a field, park or beach. Within this square the teams may erect their tents and fire up their smoker, which must be of the offset or 'barrel' type and use wood or charcoal; in fact gas or electric grills aren't normally allowed.

Charcoal and/or aromatic woods pellets are loaded into the firebox whilst the 'rubbed' meats are placed into the smoke box

or cooking chamber. These come in all shapes and sizes, from the futuristic 'Green Egg'-style smokers to retro-barrel cookers and elaborate trailer contraptions that look like steam trains!

There are usually four categories of competition: chicken, pork ribs, beef brisket and pork shoulder, also known as 'Boston butt'. Sometimes there are additional categories for spit roasting a whole hog, a speciality sauce, a signature side dish or a dessert, whilst some competitions offer an open dish category where barbecuers can let their imaginations run wild.

Any cut of meat is generally allowed in the chicken and brisket categories; however, bone-in pork ribs must be used in the rib category and a 2.3kg (5lb) or larger 'Boston butt' is required for the pork category. The rules also state that you're not allowed to do anything to your chicken, beef or pork before you arrive, but once the meat has been inspected and registered you can marinate it how you wish and start cooking.

Smoking each meat often takes several hours, as the maxim 'low and slow' is never more important than in a contest. Serious competitors will stay up all night maintaining the fire, monitoring internal temperatures and basting, spraying, mopping and wrapping. All this is essential to ensure the meats are at their best for the judging or 'turn-in'. I usually fire up my smoker at about 11pm and will often cook the brisket and pork butt for 12 to 16 hours at 110°C (230°F). However, some teams cook at 230°C (450°F) and have the brisket cooked in just five to six hours. Which method is better? Well, that's for the judges to decide!

Once cooking is finished, several samples of each meat are placed on a bed of parsley or lettuce in an insulated box. Then it's a mad dash to get your entry to the judges' tent five minutes before each meat's assigned judging time. Each category is judged at half-hour intervals, so chicken must be turned in at 12pm, ribs at 12:30pm, pork at 1pm and so on.

Judging is generally undertaken by five certified BBQ judges (CBJs) who 'blind taste' six entries each and award marks out of nine for taste, texture and appearance. A large appetite is compulsory for judges, as they'll each consume over 2lb of meat during the event! Judging is taken very seriously and the CBJs cannot fraternise with the teams, talk to other judges whilst sampling the food or even lick their fingers.

Each piece of meat is judged on its own merit and marks are awarded according to a grading scale, which starts with a median

Ben (left) at the Jack Daniel's World Championship Invitational in Tennessee, where he won the 'I Know Jack... About Grilling' category.

of six and goes from two to nine – nine being excellent and two being inedible. Each judge has previously attended a qualifying course and will know exactly how the meat should be cooked. Garnish is deliberately kept to a minimum, as the whole point is for the judges to taste the meat, not any surrounding salad.

Each category may also have its own guidelines, for example when a judge bites into a rib they should leave two white teeth marks on the bone and remove a semi-circular morsel no bigger than the size of their normal bite. Meat falling off the bone will be classed as overcooked.

When all the tasting is done, the points are tallied and prizes awarded for the top ten winners in each category. Finally an overall prize is awarded for a combination of the four meat categories. The ribbons, cups, plaques and prize money handed out can be worth thousands of dollars to the winner.

Happily you don't have to be an American to compete in the USA, and after you've sharpened your skills in a few UK cook-offs I thoroughly recommend crossing the Atlantic to compete in a big event in the spiritual home of barbecuing. Better still, why not train to be a certified BBQ judge, then you can taste some of the best barbecued food in the world for free!

So if you want to take your grill cooking to a higher level, entering a contest is definitely something you should consider. But be warned – competitive barbecuing can become highly addictive!

Glossary

Asado

A large T-shaped frame on which Argentine gauchos would barbecue huge slabs of meat. Smaller versions are now available for domestic use.

Barabicu

A cooking pit used by the indigenous peoples of Florida.

Bark

An American term for the crunchy outer layer produced when meat caramelises.

Braai

A gridiron placed over a metal trough used to cook meat in South Africa.

Baste

To moisten at intervals while cooking with a brush or spoon.

Blower fan

An appliance to quickly bring charcoal to the required cooking temperature.

Broiling

American term for grilling, usually by a hot direct heat. Pan broiling is cooking through hot dry metal over direct heat.

Bulgogi

Korean 'fire meat', prepared by marinating thin slices of meat and cooking on a grill on the diner's table.

Caramelise

Cooking until the sugars become golden brown.

Charcoal

Small pieces of wood or carbon which have been converted to char (burned in the absence of oxygen). The most common form is briquettes, which are the second most famous invention of Henry Ford.

Charred

Food cooked on the barbecue until the surface is slightly blackened.

Churrasco –

Technically grilled beef, but any meat can be part of a churrasco barbecue. Brazilian in origin.

Chimenea/Chiminea

A free-standing outdoor oven originating from Mexico, made up of a round cooking chamber and a chimney.

Cilantro

The American and Mexican term for coriander.

Cold smoking

Heating woodchips in a metal pan over heat to produce smoke without flame. Cold smoking preserves food whilst adding flavour, but without cooking. A process best left to commercial smokehouses.

Cruibins

A fancy word for grilled pigs trotters.

Diced

Food chopped into small evenly-sized cubes.

Direct heat

Cooking directly over the heat source.

Dry rub

A blend of dry spices used to enhance the flavour of meats.

Eggplant

American name for an aubergine.

Entrecôte

Another term for sirloin steak, also known as T-bone if it's still attached to the bone.

Glaze

A thin brushing of liquid to make meat glisten.

Hangi

A Maori 'earth oven' still used today.

Hexamine cooker

Type of disposable grill used in the German military in 1936. Hexamine is a solid fuel similar to paraffin wax. Domestic 'hexi-cookers' are now available from camping shops.

Horno

A beehive-shaped clay oven from North Africa.

Hot smoking

Heating woodchips in a metal pan over heat to produce smoke without flame. Hot smoking does this by restricting the flow of air and cooks food at the same time. A suitable method for amateur smokers.

Indirect heat

Cooking food in one part of a smoker barbecue, or opposite, but not directly over, flames or coals. Best for large cuts of meat or bone-in poultry.

Infuse

To extract flavour and aroma by covering a food with liquid and allowing it to stand.

Inject

To inject meats with flavoured liquids prior to cooking.

Kebab

Meat, poultry, fish, vegetables or fruit on a skewer. Wooden skewers should be soaked in water for 30 minutes prior to grilling to stop the wood from burning.

Langoustine

A large prawn, but smaller than a lobster.

Luau

A Hawaiian 'earth oven' still used today.

Maillard reaction

The scientific term for what makes food taste good! A form of non-enzymatic browning similar to caramelisation, resulting from a chemical reaction between an amino acid and reducing sugar, requiring heat. The browning of steak is an example.

Marinate

To soak food in a mixture of liquid and spices prior to cooking. Helps tenderise and add flavour.

Mesquite

The wood from this tree is used in smoker boxes to add a nutty flavour to food. Also known as Texas ironwood.

Natural lump charcoal

Hardwood char in its natural form. Burns cleaner and hotter than briquettes.

Pimento

Pepper – red, yellow or green sweet pepper, and also includes hot chilli peppers.

Pit

American name for barbecue cooking unit.

Purée

Food liquidised, blended or processed to a liquid pulp.

Raclette

A hot stone, prevalent in France and Switzerland, used for melting cheese.

Reduce

To boil a liquid in an uncovered pan so that the liquid evaporates. The mixture will thicken and the flavour will be more concentrated.

Rest

After cooking, allow meat to sit for a period of time, covered, before it's cut or sliced. This helps the muscle fibres relax and retain the juices when cut.

Rotisserie

A rotating spit for cooking meat. Often integrated with charcoal or gas grills, but you can buy a separate spit-roast attachment.

Rub

A dry mixture of sugar, salt, herbs and spices rubbed into the meat flesh.

Salsa

Literally 'sauce', often made with tomatoes and peppers, and often accompanying Mexican or Spanish food.

Satay

A Southeast Asian dish – small pieces of marinated meat grilled on a skewer.

Schwenker

A type of barbecue originating from Germany, using a round gridiron suspended from a tripod over a fire.

Score

Using a knife to make crossed-pattern incisions into meat or fish, which helps to ensure thick sections of the food are cooked evenly.

Searing

The short application of a very hot heat to the surface of meat, which seals in the natural juices and caramelises the surface, creating a flavoursome edge.

Shred

Cutting food into small narrow strips by hand, grater, or food processor. Cooked meat can be 'pulled' with two forks.

Shrimp

American word for prawn.

Smoke

Adding flavoured woodchips or blocks to a barbecue to produce smoke that can cook or partially cook and impart an extra smoky flavour to food.

Spatchcock

A way of preparing a chilcken so it cooks evenly on a grill or barbecue by spreading it open and inserting two crossed skewers to ensure it remains flat (see page 122)

Trussing

Tying up meat for cooking.

Vinaigrette

A dressing for salad with a base of oil and vinegar.

Yardbird

Barbecue competition jargon for chicken.

Zip-lock bags

Polythene bags with zip fastening, ideal for marinading.

Useful websites and telephone numbers

TV

BBC Food
www.bbc.co.uk/food

Channel 4 Food
www.channel4.com/food

Organisations

Seafish Industry Authority
www.seafish.org

Quality Standard Beef & Lamb
www.simplybeefandlamb.co.uk

Red Tractor Consumer Site
www.myredtractor.co.uk

Thanks to MJ Dalton, family butchers in Bristol, for supplying the meat www.mjdaltonbutchers.vpweb.co.uk

Beef, Pork & Lamb Information Site
www.meatmatters.com

Quality Pork Site
www.lovepork.co.uk

The Vegetarian Society
www.vegsoc.org

The British BBQ Association
www.bbqa.co.uk

Kansas City Barbeque Society
www.kcbs.us

World Barbecue Association
www.wbqa.com

National Barbecue Association
www.nbbqa.org

Equipment & fuel

Garden Furniture & Grillstream Technology Barbecues
www.leisuregrow.com
01462 744500

Crown Verity Commercial Barbecues
www.rhhall.com
01296 663400

Catering Clothing & Equipment
www.russums-shop.co.uk
0845 094 2030

Barbecue Lodges
www.bbqlodges.co.uk
01984 624040

Superfast Thermapen Temperature Thermometer
www.thermapen.co.uk
01903 202151

Jundor Barbecue Blower
www.jundor.co.uk

Kitchenware & barbecue equipment

www.lakeland.co.uk
01539 488100

Mac's BBQ Ltd (smokers)
www.macsbbq.co.uk
0845 519 4783

Barbecues and Accessories
www.socal.co.uk
02380 788155

Dingley Dell wood fired ovens
www.dingley-dell.com
01905 621636

Weber Barbecues
www.weberbbq.co.uk
01756 692600

Hot & Cold Food Smokers
www.hotsmoked.co.uk
01398 351604

Gloven Oven Gloves
www.gloven.co.uk
0800 779 7051

Gourmet Wood Chunks,
Wood Chips & Smokin' Dust Products
www.smokinlicious.co.uk

English Charcoal
www.tregothnanshop.co.uk

Foods

Fish Delivery
www.thefishsociety.co.uk
01428 687768

Seafood Delivery
www.seafooddirect.co.uk
01472 210147

Thanks also to The Fish Shop in Bristol for guidance and fish supplies
www.glosroadfish.co.uk

Organic Food Boxes
www.riverford.co.uk
01803 762059

High Quality Meat Delivery
www.donaldrussell.com
01467 629666

Herbs & Spices Manufacturer
www.britishpepper.co.uk

Organic Food
www.graigfarm.co.uk
01686 627979

Olive Oils & Mediterranean Produce
www.getoily.com
01460 242588

Index

Author's acknowledgements

I'd like to thank everyone who contributed to this book, especially Louise McIntyre (project manager for Haynes), Guy Harrop (photographer), Philip Anderton from my home town of Bristol, The Fish Shop and M.J. Dalton Butchers, my parents for doing a 'Ground Force' on my garden for the photos, and most of all to you for buying it.